Sharing the Dance

New Directions in Anthropological Writing
History, Poetics, Cultural Criticism

George E. Marcus, Rice University
James Clifford, University of California, Santa Cruz
General Editors

Cynthia J. Novack

Sharing the Dance,

Contact Improvisation and American Culture

The University of Wisconsin Press

The University of Wisconsin Press
114 North Murray Street
Madison, Wisconsin 53715

3 Henrietta Street
London WC2E 8LU, England

5 4 3 2 1

Printed in the United States of America

Library of Congress Cataloging-in-Publication Data
Novack, Cynthia Jean.
  Sharing the dance: contact improvisation and American culture /
Cynthia J. Novack.
   276 pp.   cm.—(New directions in anthropological writing)
   Includes bibliographical references.
1. Improvisation in dance—History.   2. Dancing—United States—
Anthropological aspects.   I. Title.   II. Series.
GV1781.2.N68   1990
792.8—dc20   89-40534
ISBN 0-299-12440-1   CIP
ISBN 0-299-12444-4 (pbk.)

FOR MY MOTHER
AND IN MEMORY OF MY FATHER

Contents

Contents

Illustrations

Acknowledgments

When I was considering entering a doctoral program in anthropology at Columbia University, the first person I met was Alexander Alland, Jr., then chair of the department. Upon learning that I was a dancer, he told me that he had great interest in the arts, and that, in fact, he and his wife, Sonia, had just taken a workshop in contact improvisation taught by Steve Paxton. At the time, I had no idea how involved I would come to be in this dance form as part of my work in anthropology.

During my graduate study and my eventual dissertation research and writing, Professors Alland, Robert Murphy, Katherine Newman, Abraham Rosman, and Paula Rubel were particularly helpful to me, offering inspiring intellectual guidance and encouragement throughout. The study of anthropology has been a profound gift, and I continue to be thrilled by the challenges and possibilities it holds.

The assistance and support of many other people have contributed to my work. Cogent comments on my completed dissertation manuscript were given by my dance studies colleagues of many years, Susan Foster and Susan Manning, who have also substantially influenced my ideas. George Russell, Marcia Siegel, and Hervé Varenne made perceptive suggestions for revision of the dissertation, as did series editor for the University of Wisconsin Press, James Clifford.

As I worked on writing this book, a number of people read and commented on sections or chapters from it, helping me to address important issues and to shape the text more clearly: Irene Dowd, Robert Ellis Dunn, Mark Franko, Katherine Newman, and Jill D. Sweet. Ann Daly helped edit portions of the manuscript which were published in *The Drama Review* (T120, Winter 1988). Entire versions of the manuscript were read by Joan Dulchin and Susan Foster, both of whom provided valuable suggestions. Through all the stages of writing, my husband, Richard Bull, read and discussed more pages than he must care to remember; his creative thinking, skilled editing, and irrepressible humor have been indispensable to me.

In the production stage, Kate Schellenbach at Bettmann Newsphotos and Mary Ann Jensen at the Princeton Library assisted my search for photographs. Many people at the University of Wisconsin Press contributed to the book. In particular, I am grateful to acquisitions editor Gordon Lester-Massman, my copy editor, Robin Whitaker, Carol Olsen, and my general editor, Elizabeth Steinberg, who was wonderfully perceptive and attentive in her work with me. In addition, I wish to thank James Clifford and George Marcus for their support for this kind of ethnographic subject and writing.

Two other groups of people who made this book possible must also be acknowledged. First, many individuals have sustained my education in dance. My family, especially my parents, Dora and Mendel Cohen, provided years of loving support and interest. Among my teachers, Carmen Thomas True, David Wood and Marni Thomas, Margaret Jenkins, Merce Cunningham, and Viola Farber were key in helping me to learn about dancing. So were numerous students I have taught over the years, particularly in my classes at the State University of New York–Brockport, Barnard College, and Wesleyan University's Graduate Liberal Studies Program. Experiences with a number of different colleagues have influenced and broadened my knowledge, but in particular, the years of improvising and performing with my remarkable partners, Peentz Dubble and Richard Bull, have been central to my ability to write this book.

Second, many people associated with contact improvisation enabled me to study their dancing and generously assisted me. Robin Feld, Danny Lepkoff, Nina Martin, Lisa Nelson, Nancy Stark Smith, and Randy Warshaw taught me contact improvisation. The *Contact Quarterly* office gave me access to archives, and Nancy Stark Smith spent hours of time searching for and checking information. Numerous people provided me with interview time, wrote letters and sent tapes, and tracked down photographs and other material. In addition to the dancers already mentioned and/or whose names appear in the text and legends, Carol Auerbach, Laurie Booth, Barbara Bourget, Julie Carr, Ann Cooper Albright, Juliette Crumb, Margaret Flinter, Paul Freundlich, Christine Gaigg, Alan Gardner, Naomi Goldberg, K. J. Holmes, Jack Jaeger, Marie-Stephane

Ledoux, Robbie Lehmann, Jim Lobley, Susan Lourie, Susan Milani Lauri Nagel, Rebecca Nordstrom, Anne Patz, Cheryl Pleskow, Judith Ren-Lay, Dorothea Rust, Pierre Paul Savoie, Elizabeth Smullins, Carrie Stern, and Felice Wolfzahn gave assistance.

Most important, I am grateful to Steve Paxton and to all the people who have created and continue to create this fascinating dance form. I hope that many of you feel your voices can be heard and your dancing imagined in this book.

Cynthia Novack

New York City, August, 1989

Sharing the Dance

1

Contact Improvisation
and Anthropological Analysis

Two young men, dressed in loose-fitting T-shirts and draw-string pants, roll and slide on the floor, moving in close proximity but not looking directly at each other. Although one is small and compact, the other taller and more gangly, both move with the same kind of careful languor, a deliberateness which is at once efficient and casual. They circle closer together. The shoulder of one brushes against the back of another, head touches head, hip rests momentarily against leg, and suddenly (it seems), the larger man is supported on the other's back, his weight suspended easily, his arms dangling.

The supporting figure shifts slightly, and his partner tumbles smoothly to the floor; the two, enmeshed but not entangled, roll and slide over each other now, exchanging support like two friendly wrestlers whose desire is to keep moving rather than to pin the opponent. Now they are standing, leaning against each other, still not looking into the other's face; with a sudden leap, the smaller man launches himself into the air. His partner steps quickly underneath him to break his fall, becoming a kind of moving post around which he spirals in his descent.

Contact improvisation, the dance form in which these two men are engaged, first developed in the early '70s in America. It was one of a number of enterprises during the late '60s and early '70s in dance, theater, therapy, and athletics which were trying to realize a redefinition of self within a responsive, intelligent body. Contact improvisation also formed part of social experiments in egalitarianism and communality occurring in many kinds of social and political organizations.

This ethnographic history seeks to understand contact improvisation as part of culture, to see the changes in it as revealing and commenting

1. A contact improvisation duet (Danny Lepkoff and Scott Jones). Photo © 1975 by Beatriz Schiller.

on transitional moments in recent American history. It seeks to investigate the complex, often problematic nature of this artistic and social movement and to suggest some of the different perspectives from which it might be situated in people's lives in America.

In order to perceive contact improvisation as culture, as I am proposing, it is necessary to move away from pervasive notions of mind and body

2. Nita Little and Steve Paxton. Photo © 1977 by Stephen Petegorsky.

3. A contact improvisation class doing a demonstration-performance. Photo © 1985 by Bill Arnold.

which radically separate dance from other kinds of activities and events. A brief story points to some of the issues at stake: A made-for-television movie shown in the fall of 1986 concerned the accidental deaths of two young women. The first, pronounced "body-dead" by her doctors, still has a living, functioning brain, while the second, deemed "brain-dead," continues to breathe and have an intact, functioning body. In a miracle operation, doctors place the living brain of the first woman in the living body of the second woman, and the ensuing television drama explores the question of this new person's identity.

The doctors have no problems whatsoever with the woman's identity. Gleeful over their accomplishment, they reassure her that she really is her brain and that her body is essentially irrelevant to who she is. However, her husband resists this new body and is disturbed by the fact that the woman looks, moves, and feels totally different physically; how can she be his wife? His rejection causes her to feel doubt and confusion as to her own identity. Further complications ensue. She is followed around by the husband of the woman whose body her brain now inhabits. She *looks* like his wife; she must *be* his wife, still alive somehow. Eventually, though, the miracle woman and her husband (that is, the husband of the woman whose brain now inhabits a new body) become reconciled to her new body when they both realize that, indeed, she is her brain. They all live, we assume, happily ever after.

This rather bizarre drama exemplifies some familiar attitudes toward the nature of the mind, body, and movement. Like the doctors in the television movie, many cultural observers and researchers ignore the body and its actions, seeing them as irrelevant trappings for the mind. They scarcely notice the body, seldom comment on movement, and thus often miss the role or significance of either in human events; such omissions are common in accounts of cultural history and anthropology.

If researchers do pay attention to movement and the body, it may be only in order to see the "mind" which lies behind it. If gestures, for instance, can be translated into verbal messages, then they have been "explained." Cultural observers with this orientation look for the cognitive components of movement systems (what does the movement stand for?— a common approach in popular nonverbal communication theory) and/ or the social structural implications of the body (how do concepts of the body reflect the social order?—the approach of social theorists such as Mary Douglas). These translations of movement into cognitive systems can be insightful and illuminating. However, sometimes the translations subsume the reality of the body, as if the experiences people have of themselves moving in the world were not an essential part of their consciousness and of the ways in which they understand and carry out their lives.

On the other hand, researchers who wish to redress the imbalance of mind over body may react by positing the body and movement as the primary reality. Like the husbands in the television story, they maintain the dichotomy between mind and body by emphasizing the body alone. Some researchers tend to look only "at the movement itself" ("Just describe what you see," they say) as if the body, movement, and mind were independent entities, scarcely connected to social and cultural ideas, interactions, and institutions. Indeed, a simple, descriptive approach to discussing movement characterizes much writing in dance history.

The problem here is that the division of mind and body (and the various attitudes towards movement this division suggests) dichotomizes aspects of experience which are not only closely related but which also reflect and refract one another. To detach one aspect from another for analytical purposes can contribute valuable insights into the nature of movement, but if one aspect is taken as the whole, distortion results. For in fact, as sociologist John O'Neill comments, *"Society is never a disembodied spectacle*. We engage in social interaction from the very start on the basis of sensory and aesthetic impressions" (1985:22, emphasis in original).

Culture is embodied. A primary means of understanding, knowing, making sense of the world comes through shared conceptions of our bodies and selves and through the movement experiences society offers us. Movement constitutes an ever-present reality in which we constantly participate. We perform movement, invent it, interpret it, and reinterpret it, on conscious and unconscious levels. In these actions, we participate in and reinforce culture, and we also create it. To the degree that we can grasp the nature of our experience of movement, both the movement itself and the contexts in which it occurs, we learn more about who we are and about the possibilities for knowingly shaping our lives. In this study of contact improvisation, the history of the dancing serves as a vehicle for investigating the powerful interrelationships of body, movement, dance, and society.

Contact Improvisation: An Introduction

Contact improvisation is most frequently performed as a duet, in silence, with dancers supporting each others' weight while in motion. Unlike wrestlers, who exert their strength to control a partner, contact improvisers use momentum to move in concert with a partner's weight, rolling, suspending, lurching together. They often yield rather than resist, using their arms to assist and support but seldom to manipulate. Interest lies in the ongoing flow of energy rather than on producing still pictures, as in ballet; consequently, dancers doing contact improvisation would just as soon fall as balance. Although many contact improvisers demonstrate gymnastic ability, their movement, unlike that of most gymnastic routines, does not emphasize the body's line or shape. Even more important, they improvise their movement, inventing or choosing it at the moment of performance.

The participants in contact improvisation have characterized the dance as an "art-sport," a dance form which simultaneously provides a communal movement experience for the participants and an example of movement behavior for the audience. The dancers in contact improvisation focus on the physical sensations of touching, leaning, supporting, counterbalancing, and falling with other people, thus carrying on a physical dialogue.

One contact improviser has described the dance form as "a cross between jitterbugging, wrestling, and making love." This phrase captures

4. Dena Davida, *above*, and Sylvie St. Laurent rely more on their sense of touch than on vision to dance together. Davida arches backward, guiding her movement through the sensations of contact with her partner and the floor. Photo © 1982 by André Denis.

5. A trio plays with balancing their weight, two people supporting a third with a combination of hands, feet, and knee Courtesy of Daniel Lepkoff.

6. Steve Paxton "flies," momentarily lifted by his mutual momentum with Curt Siddall. Photo © 1976 by Uldis Ohaks.

some of the influences combined in contact improvisation: it drew in its formation from social dance, sport and martial arts, and intimate, personal interaction. It also constitutes a part of the development of modern dance in America, that oppositional artistic and social movement which emerged at the beginning of the twentieth century.

Modern dancer Steve Paxton "invented" contact improvisation in 1972, giving a name to movement ideas that he had been investigating with colleagues and students. The naming both described the formal experiment and acknowledged the formation of a group of people who practiced the dance socially and performed it publicly. When the original dancers dispersed and taught contact improvisation elsewhere, larger numbers of people began to participate in cities throughout the United States, Canada, and Europe (although until the mid-'80s, most of the teachers and leaders of contact improvisation were Americans).

The people creating contact improvisation during the '70s were for the most part young, college-educated, white, middle-class Americans living in transient, communal settings. While the experiments with the movement developed, participants and viewers began to see the dancing as an expression of a way of life with certain values. The body, the primary focus of contact improvisation, became imbued with specific meanings. Contact improvisers have seen the body as a sensuous, intelligent, natural part of each person, requiring acknowledgement and promising insight.

Traditional modern dance concerns with the choreographic shaping of movement materials or with the explicit expression of ideas or emotions have often been absent from contact improvisation; emphasis has been placed instead on the physical dialogue of two dancers, the action which results from the sensations of touch and weight. Many contact improvisers have trained in modern dance; however, they frequently have looked for inspiration and ideas to physical techniques such as Tai Chi Chuan or aikido, both Asian martial arts, or to movement techniques based on kinesiology, rather than to traditional modern dance techniques based on expressive vocabularies.

Contact improvisers have often stressed the social nature of their activity as much as its formal, physical properties. Unlike other American theater dance forms, contact improvisation was and is often practiced by groups of people in informal, open social settings ("jams"). Contact improvisers, particularly during the first ten years of the form, have sometimes claimed their dancing is a kind of folk dance, something that anyone can participate in and learn.

Many of the early participants, audience members, and critics felt that the movement structure of contact improvisation literally embodied the social ideologies of the early '70s which rejected traditional gender roles and social hierarchies. They viewed the experience of touching and sharing weight with a partner of either sex and any size as a way of constructing a new experience of the self interacting with another person. The lack of conscious compositional focus in the form represented spontaneity in life, a literal "going with the flow" of events, just as the dancers followed the flow of their physical contact. The group with no director symbolized an egalitarian community in which everyone cooperated and no one dominated. Finally, the mode of practicing and performing contact improvisation resembled a social dance, an informal gathering in which anyone could participate who wished to do so; distinctions between amateur and professional dancers were consciously ignored initially.

At the same time, the values which dancers have attributed to contact improvisation have been open in practice to flexible and/or ambivalent interpretation.[1] Individuals in different circumstances have taken the initiative of using contact improvisation to fit their personal scenarios, and

---

1. See Robert Murphy (1971) for a cogent discussion of the usefulness of distinguishing values, norms, and actions while seeking to understanding their refractory and oblique interrelationships.

contradictions inherent in the clash of certain values have been worked out (or not worked out) in various ways. How does someone exert leadership within a movement which denies it? How do people take action when the prevailing ideology is to let whatever happens, happen? How is egalitarianism maintained within an individualistic community? What happens when contact improvisers incorporate as a company and enter the dance marketplace?

In fact, by the late '70s, distinctions between amateurs and professionals began to emerge as the technique of contact improvisation became extended and refined and as performance opportunities increased. Contact improvisation companies (not-for-profit corporations) were formed around the country. The growth of the contact improvisation movement was also part of a much larger trend in American theater dance—a proliferation of choreographers and dancers in the '60s and '70s.

By the early '80s, change in contact improvisation and in American culture was evident. The dance style, which in the early years had been extremely intense, risky, uncontrolled, and inwardly focused, had become more facile, fluid, controlled, and outwardly focused. Its former mixture of participation and presentation had given way in large part to a more clearly presentational manner; yet at the same time, contact improvisation companies seldom lasted longer than four or five years. In the late 1980s many dancers continued to practice and teach the form, usually performing on an occasional, ad hoc basis, but many others studied the form as a technique to be used in other kinds of dancing. Also, groups developed which organized social dance activities featuring contact improvisation; for these groups, the emphasis was on social interaction.

Apprehending these historical changes raises larger questions about the interplay of artistic techniques with the lives of participants and audiences in artistic events. It also raises questions about the relationship of cultural ideas to social institutions and movements. Contact improvisation embodies issues which must be negotiated in American culture, concepts and practices of physical skill, art, mind, body, touch, movement, play, sexuality, freedom, and difference. As a social movement, contact improvisation documents changes in these concepts that occurred during the upheavals of the 1960s.[2] Looking at how ideas central to

2. In trying to understand a countercultural movement, I have benefited from Hervé Varenne's (1986) suggestion that American culture be viewed not as a set of concrete traits but as a series of constraints.

a historical period can surface powerfully in an aesthetic environment gives insight into what "the '60s" were in the daily behavior and thoughts of some Americans. Furthermore, people doing contact improvisation maintained a countercultural image long after the '60s as a political phenomenon had ended.[3] Contact improvisation thus provides an example of the possibilities and problems of maintaining cultural ideas and practices in the face of social change.

Anthropological Analysis:
The Body, Movement, Dance, and Society

An anthropological analysis of dance springs from several important premises. First, the body and movement, the mediums of dance, are not purely natural phenomena but are constructed, in concept and practice. Second, dance is a part of culture, both contributing and responding to larger patterns of thought and organization. Third, dance constitutes an interplay of ideas, techniques, and institutions with the lives of the people involved in creating and watching it.[4]

Many anthropological writers have analyzed patterns of movement in different cultures and interpreted those patterns as distinct cultural features.[5] Dance anthropology and dance writing influenced by this approach focus on the social and public nature of dance and the ways in which dance creates meaning.[6] Like all art, dance is at once both aesthetic and social.

3. Fredric Jameson (1984) discusses the widespread economic and political conditions which might define or "periodize" the '60s as lasting from about 1960 until 1972–74.

4. Studies of dance and dance history contain many examples of a different tradition, one that assumes that the body and movement are completely natural, rendering dance an instinctive and universal expression. Often such presentations of dance also implicitly or explicitly incorporate a nineteenth-century evolutionary description of dance history, portraying primitive dance as a more natural activity which later developed into the civilized art of the Western theater, or, conversely, presenting primitive dance as a sacred, pure activity now lost to civilization. For examples of the former, see Sachs 1963 or, more recently, Clarke and Crisp 1982:7. For an example of the latter approach, see Steinman's (1986) account of contemporary performance and dance (including contact improvisation), which tries to regain the "natural." For the classic article which critiques this point of view, see Kealiinohomoku 1969.

5. Some of the major theorists who have investigated movement as culture include Mauss (1973), Birdwhistell (1970), Hall (1969), Douglas (1982), Blacking (1977), and Scheflen (1972).

6. Many dance writers have helped to shape my understanding of dance as culture. In particular, the work of Joann Kealiinohomoku (1969, 1976), Adrienne Kaeppler (1978,

A dance performance, in this view, is always a cultural performance as well.[7] Dance constitutes a form of meaning and action, and like all culture, it is multivoiced and flexible. In the beliefs it espouses both explicitly and implicitly, dance may shape part of our definition of physical virtuosity, our concept of beauty, or our perception of meaning in movement. It may constitute part of our sense of time and space, our understanding of the construction and relationships of the body, mind, and person, or our ideas of what a man and a woman are. Dance may convey interactions of individual and group, or provide a vision of power and power relationships. And it may embody abstract patterns of space or of phrasing which constitute part of our aesthetic or cognitive sensibilities.

Dance, because it is uniquely situated in the human body as the medium for art as well as the means for it, possesses special properties as an art (and, to the extent that theater, music, poetry, or storytelling are blended with dance or movement elements, the qualities I am discussing apply to these performances as well). In particular, dance combines referential qualities—allusions to ideas and events outside of itself—with formal principles.[8] Dance contains referential qualities which are often, though not always, less explicit than those of literature or theater. Nonetheless, reference is central to dance because of the constant presence of the human body and human movement. Dance always involves an image of the person, usually of the person in relation to others and in relation to ideas, and thus social references remain implicitly ever present, even in dances which claim to be purely formal or only personally expressive.

At the same time, dance is highly formal: like music, dance organizes material through principles of rhythm, dynamics, and temporal structuring. Like the visual arts, dance shapes movement using principles of spatial design, volume, weight, and texture. Experiences with formal principles engage and influence perception, affecting the apprehension

---

1985), Jill D. Sweet (1985), Suzanne Youngerman (1983), Susan Manning (1987), and Susan Foster (1986) have been important influences.

7. Milton Singer (1972) used the term "cultural performance" to refer to events such as plays, lectures, and concerts, but also "prayers, ritual readings and recitation, rites and ceremonies, festivals, and all those things we usually classify under religion and ritual rather than with the cultural and artistic" (70–71). Contact improvisation includes things we usually classify under socializing, athletics, and therapy rather than with the cultural and artistic.

8. This particular formulation follows Leonard Meyer's analyses of Western literature, theater, music, and visual art (1965). Meyer suggests that literature is primarily both referential and syntactical, and music is primarily both syntactical and formal (112–13); I am arguing that dance is primarily both referential and formal.

of the world on many different levels—cognitive, emotional, physical. Thus, dance combines form and reference, tying formal changes in technique to changes of meaning for performer and audience through the body and movement of the performer.

In the Euro-American tradition of the rationalization of art and its separation from other aspects of social life, the social organization of art has often remained submerged and apparently unconnected to the work itself (Becker 1982; Bensman 1983; Williams 1982). Yet any art, including dance, entails social organization and must exist within economic and political structures.[9] In order to understand the development of any dance form, one must examine the interplay of different "areas" of dance, which, although theoretically separable, are in fact interacting, related, sometimes conflicting processes: (1) the technical and conceptual developments or experiments with the dance form itself; (2) the lives and perspectives of the artists/participants; (3) the responses of the viewers; and (4) the means through which dance is organized and produced.[10]

In defining the social organization of contact improvisation, I have attempted to place it as a community within a larger national context.[11] Anthropological and sociological studies of American culture have proliferated in the past thirty years, with subjects for study selected from a variety of kinds of communities—representatives of classes and of ethnic groups, neighborhoods, clubs, occupational groups, and a range of socially marginal "subcultures." Contact improvisation lends itself well to an analysis as a community; although its boundaries have not been residential, it has constituted a community of experience.

People in this community have shared a common dance form, customary ways of discussing that dance form, a publication, and an artistic

---

9. See Spencer 1985 for a collection of essays analyzing dance from a social perspective.

10. Raymond Williams' literary and cultural writing (1959, 1976, 1982) presents an important model of art criticism which considers these interrelationships. A formal innovation in art, suggests Williams, may also be a "true and integral element" of social changes themselves, "an articulation, by technical discovery, of changes in consciousness which are themselves forms of consciousness of change" (1982:142). The work of Clifford Geertz, particularly his discussions of cultural events as texts (see "Deep Play: Notes on a Balinese Cockfight" in Geertz 1973) and religion and art as cultural systems (1973, 1983), also offers valuable insights into the social meanings of aesthetic sensibility.

11. Spindler and Spindler (1983) provide an overview of the shift in the study of American culture away from "the notion of community as a bounded, isolated, and self-sufficient place towards a concept of community as a dependent part of a larger system" (49).

history traced back to a single group of people led by a single figure, Steve Paxton. They have shared common artistic ideas and, often, social ideas which in many ways have paralleled the ethos of their dancing.

At the same time, that community has by no means been isolated. Although the United States clearly encompasses a plural cultural reality, dominant national economic, political, and cultural institutions impose restrictions on community cultural developments. For an alternative art movement, the structures of the culturally dominant art institutions—the systems of legal incorporation, the operations of theaters and presenting organizations, the processes of funding and grant giving—exert powerful influence.[12] Contact improvisation has constituted a social experiment, an attempt to place dance in a liminal social context which fitted neither the category of theater dance nor the category of social dance. The successes and failures of that experimental community, as well as the nature of its internal leadership and authority, must be viewed in light of prevailing modes of organization in the American dance world and the society at large.

Moreover, "subcultures" or oppositional movements appear as an important part of American cultural patterns; the assertion of difference is quintessentially American. One might say that the basic process of Protestantism involves a breakup into denominations, each of which, eventually, closely resembles the others, but all of which continue to assert and practice their "differences" (Varenne 1977). The moment of formation of a new sect may be its most lively, truly different moment, after which the forces of institutionalization begin to exercise constraint. So, too, American modern dance developed as a series of break-away movements, each proclaiming its uniqueness and freedom from the limitations of prior movements.

Researching and Writing an Ethnographic History

The main orientation of my study of contact improvisation is qualitative, interpretive, and ethnohistorical—to describe and analyze the history of a way of life and a way of dancing as part of culture. Thus, I derived the data from activities associated with the realm of traditional anthropological fieldwork and ethnographic writing.

12. For discussions of institutional constraints and influences in the performing arts in North America and Europe, see the collections of essays edited by Kamerman and Martorella (1983), DiMaggio (1986), and Lowry (1984).

My own background crucially shaped my fieldwork experience. I am a dancer, and I have been engaged in many dance forms both as techniques for moving and as subjects for study for many years. The techniques include those of improvisational dance, modern dance, ballet, tap dance, West African dance, and popular/social dance forms. Since 1978, I have focused on choreographic performance improvisation, dancing and teaching professionally in a collaborative trio.

I first saw a contact improvisation performance in 1974 and watched others occasionally over subsequent years. While I found contact improvisation fascinating, I never became involved in trying to learn to do it myself during the '70s. My anthropological study of contact improvisation began in 1980, when I attended the annual conference of the American Dance Guild held in Minneapolis, a conference of some three hundred dancers, teachers, and students which focused on dance improvisation, including contact improvisation.

At that conference, titled Improvisation: Dance as Art-Sport, I conducted research to discern values common to improvisational dancers and to survey methods of improvisation. In the course of talking to many people, seeing performances, and participating in classes presented by dancers from all over the country, I realized that the contact improvisers constituted a clear social and artistic group, distinct from all the other improvisers at the conference. I began to perceive that contact improvisation formed a discrete, self-defined unit that could be studied by itself and that to do so would not be inventing an artificial category. Furthermore, I became excited about the questions that the practice and performance of contact improvisation implicitly raised.

At that point, I began to concentrate on contact improvisation as a subject for an anthropological study of a dance form. I studied how the form was taught (and learned) in contact improvisation classes and workshops and at informal dance sessions (jams) in New York City and in New England. I attended performances and lectures, and spoke with and observed dancers in these settings. After this preliminary research, I conducted extended interviews with a range of people involved in contact improvisation—from different "generations" and with varying degrees of involvement—and also with some people who have only watched it or heard about it. Contact improvisation occupies a unique place in the American theater dance world because its center is not in New York City. Consequently, I spoke to or corresponded with people from other parts of the United States, as well as from Canada, and from Europe. I also consulted written material about contact improvisation and studied and analyzed videotapes of performances in different stages of the development of the form.

My observations and questions were aimed at eliciting information about the participants in contact improvisation (including past and present associations with other forms of dance, and histories of their involvement with contact improvisation), and about the history of the development of the form as it was theorized about, practiced, taught, performed, and watched. I also collected information about the nature of the social networks of contact improvisation, the nature of leadership within the movement, and the relationship of the contact improvisation community to the modern dance community and to teaching, granting, and presenting organizations.

In writing my ethnographic history, I had to determine what kind of a history to write. I have focused on contact improvisation as a social movement composed of many people, rather than as the history of its founder. This approach coincides with recent attempts in social history to discuss movements and social groups, looking to everyday events and relationships in people's lives as repositories of larger cultural conditions. It also coincides with anthropological traditions, particularly those which have tried to combine synchronic and diachronic analyses, tracing cultural and social structures through time.[13]

At the same time, I have also written a dance history. Unlike many ethnographies, particularly those dealing with contemporary American culture, my account often supplies the names of speakers and records the people present at particular events. I decided to do this early in my fieldwork, realizing that by naming names rather than camouflaging identities, I would not be able to reveal certain information which would be personally embarrassing (for example, some criticisms of one dancer by another) or an invasion of privacy (the history of certain personal relationships).

This constraint did not always apply; many people gave permission to include their comments even though these might be considered controversial. Undoubtedly, though, censorship occurred as people talked with me and decided what they could and could not reveal. My familiarity and sympathy with dance lent me credibility and encouraged people to

13. See, for example, Marshall Sahlins 1981, 1985 and Maurice Bloch 1986 for a discussion of these issues.

give me information; at the same time, my identity as a colleague and as a dance writer constructing history also shaped our interaction.

All anthropology is characterized by self-reflexiveness, an inevitable response when one human being observes other human beings. Studying contact improvisation and carrying on a dialogue with dancers had a profound effect on me, and throughout my fieldwork and writing, I was confronted by my own relationship to contact improvisation and to the poeple who did it.

Initially, I was concerned about my personal feelings of ambivalence about the dance form. I found the movement fascinating to watch, and I admired the skill and artistry of many of the dancers. I also sometimes found the dancing limited and repetitive, in part because choreographic concerns, one of my own primary interests, seemed absent. In my first encounters with the contact improvisation movement, before I was consciously taking the point of view of an anthropologist and was simply another dancer, circumstances arose in which I grew impatient with what I perceived as the insularity and cultishness of many of the participants. But I believed that in order to begin to understand the dance form, I needed to be able to put aside my personal judgements, to listen and watch receptively, sympathetically.

I found that feelings of impatience and intolerance tended to fade as I began to study the movement and find out what was involved in doing it. Most of the contact improvisers whom I met and spoke with were very engaging, and they articulated a love of dancing which I shared. The experience of doing the form unexpectedly changed the way I danced and altered my understanding of movement. Aspects of contact improvisation began to permeate my own dancing and teaching, and differences between myself and others seemed interesting to me rather than threatening.

An opposite concern of my initial one became increasingly prominent: had I "gone native"? How could I possibly achieve the distance necessary to address a broader audience or to describe contact improvisation within larger contexts? I have always felt that much dance writing bears an uncomfortable resemblance to public relations writing; my desire to write about dance anthropologically is related to my conviction that other ways to approach the subject need to be developed. The challenge that lay before me was to present points of view of different contact improvisers while clarifying my own responses and analyses.

In the course of fieldwork, I experienced a strange sort of culture shock. By carrying on research in my own culture, I had made myself acutely aware of my different roles; for a while I was almost constantly distanced from whatever I was doing, seeing it from another perspective. Participant-observation became a condition of life.

One incident remains strong in my memory as an example of my state of mind (body) while conducting research. I was attending the Malinowski Lectures, an anthropological conference at New York University, at which three papers had been delivered. On this particular Saturday morning, a panel composed of the three speakers and three additional anthropologists responding to their papers had argued over issues and nonissues, engaging heatedly in both interesting debate and the sort of polemical one-upmanship seemingly endemic to academic discussion.

The panel was followed by a reception at which I suddenly perceived the entire crowded roomful of people as doing a strange dance. In this dance, bodies shifted in space and then maintained a relative stillness except for the heads, which moved constantly and with some agitation. As I traveled around, participating in the dance, I exchanged customary greetings with colleagues and professors—a quick hug, bodies held slightly rigid, hands clasping the other's shoulders as much to keep the person at a proper distance as to reach out.

I then left the university to walk over to the lower East Side to a public school at which Dance New England was holding a weekend session of dance. This was to be my first encounter with Dance New England, a social network built around contact improvisation; previously I had met only a few individuals who were part of it. As I approached the school, I saw a barefoot man whom I did not know, dressed in sweatpants and a bright yellow T-shirt, standing near the door. As I turned from the sidewalk, he walked forward, reached out for me, and, embracing me with the full length and a good part of the weight of his body, said, "It's wonderful to see you. Welcome." Startled, I realized that I was holding myself rigid in his embrace. Taking a deep breath, I softened myself a little and managed to mumble something along the lines of, "It's great to see you, too." Then I went inside to try to learn more about Dance New Englanders, to be the anthropologist studying the contact improvisers.

In time, I learned to make the shift easily from one culture to another, participating in the "strange" behavior of each as relatively "natural" events. Furthermore, I realized that the alternation of roles was of great benefit, enabling me to experience different perspectives while serving as a caution against getting lost in any one of them. The contrast alerted me to what was present or absent in each circumstance, enabling me to take at least a partly critical stance. I could not forget the absence of "body" in academia, the stubborn denial of the physical self. Nor could I become immune to the potentially problematic skirting of sexual/emotional boundaries in contact improvisation. The dichotomies of American culture were part of my everyday experience of fieldwork.

Clifford Geertz has argued that anthropological understanding does not result from acts of "empathy" with the "natives," leaving the ethnographer "awash in immediacies as well as entangled in vernacular." Nor does it result from distant and removed observation, leaving the ethnographer "stranded in abstractions and smothered in jargon" (1977:482). Geertz advocates use of "the hermeneutic circle" (after Dilthey), a moving back and forth or, rather, around in a spiral, between asking about natives: "'What is the general form of their life?' and 'What exactly are the vehicles in which that form is embodied?'" Both questions together, by posing a method for how to conduct analysis, demystify the ethnographer's task and also tend to move the ethnographer in a spiral between generalizations and specific observations, abstractions and immediacies, looking "from the outside" and trying to understand the vantage points "from the inside."

I have tried to travel this spiral in doing my research and in writing about it. The chapters which follow focus on particular topics and points of view, but they cross and recross the same territory repeatedly in order to "thicken the description" (Geertz 1973:14). Chapters 2, 3, and 4 set the stage, discussing the historical, choreographic, and social development of contact improvisation. Chapters 5 through 8 focus on particular aspects of this development and its implications for understanding American culture. All direct quotations in the text, unless otherwise cited, are taken from conversations and interviews conducted during my fieldwork (1980–88).

I have used photographs throughout to help describe the visual and kinesthetic characteristics of contact improvisation and other dance and movement activities, and to comment on or illustrate particular ideas in the text. The photographs, by their very nature, are representations of a moment within the flow of ongoing events and can thus be deceptive. Nevertheless, when viewed with a sense of movement in mind, they may provide a provocative counterpoint to the written text.

2
Contact Improvisation's Origins and Influences

The Heritage of Early Modern Dance

Contact improvisation developed from the tradition of modern dance, part of the twentieth-century movement of modernism in art. This tradition engaged moral and philosophical issues concerning the primacy of the individual in society and the communication of ideas and emotion. Its formal preoccupations centered around the invention of new structures and techniques which could reveal contemporary visions of life.[1]

In America, modern dance took on the character of continuing revolution, a re-creation of the American frontier standing counter to the European, aristocratic form of ballet.[2] During the 1930s, John Martin, one of the critical spokesmen for the new modern dance, proclaimed the revolutionary ideology of this undertaking: "It [the modern dance] has thrown aside everything that has gone before and started all over again from the beginning" (1968:6).[3] Martin's claim that modern dance threw aside "everything" that had gone before and started all over again

1. For accounts of this early period of modern dance in America, see Kendall 1979; Shelton 1981; and Siegel 1979.

2. As dance historian Susan Manning (1987) has pointed out, modern dance was also associated with nationalism in Europe and America, taking on different characteristics in each location as artists sought to wed their new art to national visions (19–21).

3. From a different perspective, cultural historian Warren Susman (1984) has described this same period as "the age of culture and commitment" in American life, a time characterized by the quest to define and celebrate the culture of America while seeking important and stable forms, patterns, and symbols to which one might be passionately committed (185).

"from the beginning" echoes the enduring theme of the new frontier in American history.

Structural similarities between the early formation of modern dance in the '20s and '30s and the wave of experimental dance (including contact improvisation) in the '60s and '70s point to a repeating pattern. Dancers in both periods held ideologies of social consciousness and radicalism, often intentionally establishing connections between movement ideas and social concepts. Both early modern dance and contact improvisation were experimental movements, not formalized initially, consisting largely of a set of principles or ideas about moving which people explored. Like early modern dance, which was related to physical culture movements, Delsarte training, and various theatrical genres, early contact improvisation was related to a wide variety of activities: sports (especially gymnastics), aikido, body therapies, social dance, and modern dance techniques. Finally, dancers in both periods produced their work in marginal circumstances, trying to finance their dancing while maintaining a sense of artistic independence.

While modern dancers in the '20s and '30s struggled to present their work as a serious American art form, they simultaneously professionalized it, disassociating modern dance from both social dancing and entertainment dance (vaudeville, for example). As "art," the new dance did not draw large audiences, and the modern dance tradition consolidated as a spiritual, artistic endeavor performed because of love and dedication to the ideals of dance.

In addition, the development of group choreography necessitated the establishment of schools for training dancers and of modern dance companies for presenting performance. In the company, the individual choreographer was conceived of as the creative source of the work executed by the dancers, as the person who shaped and set the work of art until it was ready to be presented before an audience. The dancers were, in theory at least, dedicated to the individual choreographic and artistic vision of their director and united by a belief in the artistic and spiritual value of their activity.

Concomitantly, these choreographers considered improvisation part of the process of discovery of movement, a tool for choreography and not part of the finished product.[4] While improvisation became the method

4. In practice, both choreographic contributions by dancers and extemporaneous movement in performance occurred, but they were largely acknowledged privately. For a rare public acknowledgment of such occurrences, see Paul Taylor's account of working with Martha Graham in *Private Domain* (1987:117–18).

for the teaching of creative, educational dance in colleges and recreational programs, the categories of education and art remained separate, implicitly associating improvisation with amateur self-expression. The only major exception to the absence of improvisation from the early American modern dance tradition was the teaching of Hanya Holm, expatriate student of the German dancer Mary Wigman. In Germany, modern dancers always considered improvisational practices to constitute part of their technical training; Holm continued teaching improvisation and composition in America, as did her students Alwin Nikolais and Murray Louis. Yet even in this professional technique, improvisation has still been a part of the training method, not a vehicle for performance.

The heritage of early modern dance was maintained historically through institutions of teaching and performing, which became extensively developed during the '30s and '40s. Choreographers transmitted particular movements from dance techniques and the ethos and structures of modern dance practice. Many maintained schools or classes in New York and other cities. Some traveled around the country, performing and teaching. Former members of their companies and students who had trained in their schools staffed many of the dance programs in colleges and universities. During the period following World War II, any student of modern dance, as opposed to ballet, encountered the aesthetic philosophies and movement techniques of those who consolidated early modern dance: Martha Graham, Doris Humphrey and Charles Weidman, Lester Horton, Helen Tamiris, Hanya Holm, Katherine Dunham. Although students may have been unaware of the historical conditions under which modern dance developed, the teaching they experienced was imbued with images of individualism, pioneering innovation, and emotional expression realized in the physical technique and choreographic ideas of one or another of these pioneers.

Many of the dancers who were to participate in the experiments of the '60s studied this modern dance tradition. Many of them also experienced changes and new developments occurring in dance, changes which eventually affected ideas and techniques of dance in the '60s and the initiation of contact improvisation. Because continuities and transformations in concepts of dance and dancing during the postwar period occurred in the actual practice of dance, it is helpful to examine the work of people who were teaching and choreographing in the late '40s and throughout the '50s. The aesthetic philosophies of three teachers and choreographers exemplary of the period—Merce Cunningham, Anna

Halprin, and Erick Hawkins—illuminate some of the particular concepts being explored at the time which eventually figured prominently in the development of contact improvisation. The following discussion of these artists (all of whom were still active teachers and choreographers in 1990) selects the aspects of their work which highlight particular historical changes relevant to contact improvisation.

The Physical Reality of the Body: Merce Cunningham

Overt social and political commentary which made a statement or sent a message to the audience became much less prevalent for many artists after World War II. Merce Cunningham and other artists maintained a choreographic focus on movement which did not have a determined symbolic meaning or legibly communicative intent. These choreographers claimed to be making radical changes in modern dance, freeing it from the psychologism and social involvement of earlier dances and allowing the audience a greater freedom to interpret the dance. In an important shift of orientation, they tried to remove meaning from a symbolic or narrative content of dance and place it in the act of developing new movement techniques and/or new formal or structural methods for choreography.[5]

Merce Cunningham attempted to create a dance form in which any kind of movement could be called dance and in which the dance was not supposed to represent anything other than itself as a physical, human action.

> ". . . I don't ever want a dancer to start thinking that a movement *means* something. That was what I really didn't like about working with Martha Graham—the idea that was always being given to you that a particular movement meant something specific. I thought that was nonsense. And, you know, I really think Martha felt it was, too. . . . It's always seemed to me that Martha's followers make

---

5. The source of these changes in part derives from the imperative of modern dance to be continually innovative. Because overt political action in social arenas within the general population diminished dramatically in the cold war atmosphere of the '50s, some artists, not surprisingly, also turned away from political drama and investigated the formal aspects of art devoid of explicit commentary. Also, the growth of new media and technology exerted an impact on artistic perception. The dances of Cunningham and choreographers such as Alwin Nikolais raised questions about the relationship of modern people to their changing technological environments.

her ideas much more rigid and specific than they really are with her. . . ." (Quoted in Tomkins 1965:246–47)

Cunningham also rejected models of modern dance composition based on traditional musical forms. "'I never could stand the modern-dance idea of structure in terms of theme and variations,'" he is quoted as saying. "'That sort of A-B-A business based on emotional or psychological meanings just seemed ridiculous to me'" (Tomkins 1965:244). Instead, Cunningham presented his choreography as movement arrived at through the sole process of moving.

> "There's no thinking involved in my choreography. I work alone for a couple of hours every morning in the studio. I just try things out. And my eye catches something in the mirror, or the body catches something that looks interesting; and then I work on that. . . . I don't work through images or ideas—I work through the body." (Tomkins 1965:246)

Cunningham sometimes employed chance procedures. The idea of using chance came from John Cage, who, influenced by his study of Zen Buddhism, adopted chance in his music as a means of "removing" himself "from the activities of the sounds" he made and avoiding musical habits. Thus, sound could emerge by a random process which Cage thought more in keeping with process in nature (1966:9–10). For Cunningham, Calvin Tomkins explains, chance "sometimes (but not always) enters the choreographic process as a means of determining the kinds of movement used, the order of the movements, the tempi, and other specific aspects of the dance; Cunningham uses it to arrive at certain decisions, which are then permanent" (1965:275).

As with most human endeavors, differences exist between what Cunningham actually did in his dances and his account of what he did.[6] There is a remarkable continuity, however, in the way in which Cunningham explains and conceives of dancing and the way in which many contact improvisers understand their dancing.[7] Neither Cunningham nor someone

6. In a fascinating interview by David Vaughan (Vaughan et al. 1987), seven former Cunningham dancers, including Steve Paxton, discuss the choreographer's work as they experienced it. They assert the narrative and imagistic content of Cunningham's dances, and they clearly explain his use of chance procedures.

7. For further discussion of Cunningham and his choreography and philosophy, see Cage 1966; Cunningham 1968, 1985; Johnston 1976; Klosty 1975; Jowitt 1988; and "Time to Walk in Space" 1968.

7. Three couples simultaneously engage in different activities during a moment in Merce Cunningham's "Variations V" (1965) creating a multifocused composition. This dance was made more complex by film projections on stage (by Stan VanDerBeek) which interspersed television images (by Nam June Paik) with images of the dancers, and by a sound score (by John Cage) generated by amplifying the sounds of the dancers' feet on the floor. As in many of Cunningham's works, the actions are a mixture of "dancerly" and "pedestrian," or tasklike, movements; at one point in this piece, Cunningham rode a bicycle around the stage. *From left to right,* the dancers are Sandra Neels, Albert Reid, Gus Solomons, Jr., Carolyn Brown, Barbara Dilley (Lloyd), and Peter Saul. Photo © 1965 by Peter Moore.

doing contact improvisation suggests choreography as a highly conceptual, conscious, intentional process. They describe it emerging from the act of moving, the body, not the mind, producing it. Also, in this view of dance, choreography happens to a greater degree by accident than as a result of human will.

Major differences exist between Cunningham's choreography and contact improvisation. The movement characteristics contrast markedly. Cunningham rejected improvisation, occasionally opting for indeterminacy (as in "Story" and "Field Dances" [1963]) but for the most part maintaining the set nature of the choreographic product.[8] He also followed the traditional social arrangement of the company led by the single choreographer, whereas contact improvisation has not. But Cunningham, by stripping dance of its intentionally symbolic or narrative content, by rejecting traditional methods of composition, and by focusing on the physical activity of moving as the content of the dance, suggested ways to alter the meaning of the dance.

Improvisation and the Theater of the Body: Anna Halprin

The work of San Francisco choreographer Anna Halprin provides a second example of experiments in modern dance which became widespread during the '60s and which influenced the development of contact improvisation. Halprin became interested in constructing improvisational structures for performance as an alternative to setting every movement beforehand. She saw improvisation as a means to both personal development and collaboration among dancers (Hartman 1977–78).[9]

Through improvisation, Halprin extended the modernist notion of "subjectivity." Whereas subjectivity had formerly applied to the choreographer's investigation, in improvisational work each dancer explored his or her own subjectivity. Halprin claimed she turned to improvisation in order to figure out "how one could move if you weren't Doris Humphrey and you weren't Martha Graham, but you were just Anna Halprin" (Halprin 1980).[10]

She also saw improvisation as a way of including the audience in the performance, overcoming the common division of participants at a performance into "specialists and gawkers." Because choreographers typically use improvisation only in rehearsal to help create a set product to be placed before an audience, Halprin thought, "the audience can only share in the product and that is why they become gawkers." On the other hand, "improvisation has the possibility of making process visible" to the

8. In indeterminate art, some events are allowed to occur by spontaneous accident or random choice, rather than as a result of active design. Indeterminacy could be categorized as a very particular kind of improvisation; only in this sense could one say that Cunningham ever used improvisation.

9. See also Halprin 1965 and 1967–68.

10. Interestingly, Halprin studied under Margaret H'Doubler, the dance educator who started the first college dance major in America at the University of Wisconsin in 1926 (Morrison 1973). Halprin credits H'Doubler with introducing her to improvisation (1965).

audience (Halprin 1980). Some of Halprin's works were scores which actually included the audience as participants in the dance.

Halprin sought to generate movement outside of traditional dance techniques. One source of movement derived from interactive improvi-

8. John Graham and A. A. Leah investigate their relationship using movement and a radio as a prop in Anna Halprin's "Apt. 6" (1965). In the '60s, Halprin's work was considered as much "theater' as "dance," but however she was categorized, her firm basis in movement as a source and motivation for human action remained. Photo by Warner Jepson. Courtesy of Anna Halprin.

sational structures: John LeFan, a student of Halprin's who later became a contact improviser, recalled one of her exercises called "Wonderworm," an improvisation for a large group of people giving and taking weight. Improvisation also became a way for expanding range of movement, rather than confining it to a codified vocabulary. For example, Halprin might instruct students to run "while moving the spine through any possible positions." Movement in nature fascinated Halprin, providing another source from which to derive different movement vocabulary, as did everyday, "pedestrian" movement. Through the particular combination of her teaching techniques and interests, Halprin identified improvisation with natural action and with everyday interaction. She also emphasized the direct, sensuous experience of movement, instructing students to experience "kinesthetic awareness" and sense the "body's changing dynamic configurations" (Forti 1974:29–31). Emphasis in training often lay on the experience of movement to a much greater degree than on the appearance.

Halprin has been an influential teacher on the West Coast, and many of her students participated in experimental dance and theater in the '60s, in California, New York, and elsewhere. Her work informed the investigation of improvisation in the '60s, the concern with ritual and body awareness, and the interest in therapeutic aspects of movement. The relationship of Halprin's work to contact improvisation is clear: it involved improvisation, lessening the control of the choreographer; it emphasized kinesthetic awareness and moving in a "natural" way; and it occurred outside of New York City. By combining improvisational methods with conceptions of a natural basis for movement, Halprin contributed to a concept of theater based on interaction and on the impulses of the body.

Science and Sensuality: Erick Hawkins

Choreographer Erick Hawkins pursued dance ideas in the postwar period which exemplified changing concepts about movement, particularly those which concerned methods of training the body. He studied kinesiology, including the work of Mabel Ellsworth Todd ([1937] 1972) and Lulu Sweigard (1974), as well as writings in dance, philosophy, and religion, especially Zen Buddhism. From these studies, Hawkins developed a philosophy of movement training which emphasized sensations of moving combined with techniques seen to be based on scientific and philosophical principles.[11]

Hawkins' conception of the body can be illustrated by comparing it structurally with views of the body in several other dance forms. For example, twentieth-century ballet proposes the body as an instrument which must be trained to conform to the classical movement vocabulary. Russian critic André Levinson ([1918], 1985) argued that the beauty of ballet lay in its artificiality, in the wonder of seeing a body accomplish feats so foreign to the experience of the audience. In contrast, modern dancers in the '30s and '40s subscribed to a more expressionistic view of the body, one in which internal feelings were realized in external movement. Although the body conformed to a vocabulary, that vocabulary was thought to have a basis in a natural, universal expression of human feeling.

Dancers in the postwar period began turning to another model of the body which was at once more abstract, or objective, and more phenomenological.[12] Hawkins was one of the most articulate proponents of this view, formulating what he called a "normative," or "generic," theory of dance movement by which one could train the body in basic, scientific principles of motion, applicable to everyday life as well as to dance. This basic understanding lay the groundwork for the creation of theatrical dance (Brown 1971–72).

In Hawkins' view, the body is both a natural instrument, subject to laws of gravity and motion, and the means for experiencing the world. Zen, claimed Hawkins, encouraged him to find a way of allowing movement to happen, of learning to dance without forcing the body. Consequently, his training emphasizes "kinesthetic awareness," the sensation of movement occurring in muscles and joints, so that the body might be used efficiently and without strain or stress. At the same time, the dancer should "think-feel," Hawkins' phrase for a state of "intellectual knowing with sensuous experiencing" (Brown 1971–72:11).

Again, as with all theories of the dance, execution does not always

11. Hawkins' training methods are described by Beverly Brown (1971–72). For other discussions of Hawkins, see Pennella 1978; Elias 1978; and Hawkins 1965.

12. My characterization of different bodies is consonant with Susan Foster's (1986) analysis of four paradigms of dance represented by George Balanchine, Martha Graham, Merce Cunningham, and Deboray Hay (a contemporary of Steve Paxton's). Foster suggests that the dancer's body in Balanchine's work is "a medium for displaying ideal forms," in Graham's is "a unified vehicle for expressing the self," in Cunningham's is "bones, muscles, ligaments, nerves, etc.," and in Hay's is "a fluid aggregate of cells" (42–43).

9. Soft fluidity and lightness characterize the dance "Here and Now With Watchers" performed in 1957 by Erick Hawkins and Barbara Tucker. The dance suggests no plot, yet evokes sensuality and nature through its movement, music, and poetic program notes. Yvonne Rainer, who would become one of Steve Paxton's colleagues, wrote, "I saw 'Here and Now With Watchers' and decided to become a dancer" (1974:4). Photo by A. John Geraci. Courtesy of the Erick Hawkins Dance Company.

match idea. Just as Cunningham did not practice "all movement" even though he claimed that every movement could be dance, so Hawkins built his theatrical dance into a very particular style, an immediately recognizable technique—soft, fluid, and light yet firmly connected to the ground.[13] But an increasing number of dancers through the '60s, including people who eventually participated in contact improvisation, shared Hawkins' interest in efficient movement based on natural laws and in sensuous experiencing of movement as a primary focus for the dancer. The description of movement by contact improvisers contains the same concerns. By combining kinesiology with "felt" experience, Hawkins suggested a way to reconceive of dance technique and the sensation of dancing.

Social Dance in the '60s

Many of the dancers who were to create contact improvisation came of age in the late '50s and in the '60s. They participated in dance of the traditional modern schools as well as of the developing schools of choreographers like Cunningham, Halprin, and Hawkins. Both theatrical and social dance in this period distinctively manifested cultural and political changes. Existing techniques took on other meanings, new techniques were developed, and different attitudes emerged toward the activity of dancing.

In a conversation between choreographers Douglas Dunn and Trisha Brown, recorded in the late '70s, Dunn commented, "Before the sixties there was no consciousness of certain things as being dance." Brown added, "I think the 'Twist' helped a lot in the sixties." And Dunn replied, "Rock dancing was a bridge between your daily life, which was still unconscious perhaps, and part of your classroom dance life which was not making available that possibility [of all kinds of movement] . . ." (J. M. Brown 1979:170). Social dance exerted a powerful influence on conceptions of movement among many dancers and their audiences.

In the late '50s and early '60s in America, large numbers of people

13. These inconsistencies should not be seen as failures; rather, it seems impossible to develop a movement training without making selections. Otherwise, movement experience is so eclectic as to be without pattern, and the body never becomes constructed, physically or conceptually. Of course, differences of opinion exist as to the range of movement desirable and/or necessary to constitute a technique for dance training, but that leads to another discussion altogether.

danced to rock 'n' roll, a musical form based on rhythm and blues, jazz, and country music; the dancing itself drew heavily from African-American sources (for example, the jitterbug from the lindy, and the frug, the watusi, the mashed potato, and the funky chicken, from other black dance traditions).[14]

American blacks, and some whites, throughout American history had carried on the development of African-American dance and music forms, often adapted and synthesized with European forms. This dancing prominantly included extensive use of shoulders, head, hips, and knees, often moving independently or in different directions at the same time. Emphasis tended to be on continuity of energy flow and strong rhythmic impulses, rather than on the specific positioning of body parts, and on improvisation both by individual dancers and by couples.

Although these characteristics had influenced social dance in America in general for over a hundred years, rock 'n' roll dance marked a major, widespread incorporation of these qualities into the mainstream of American dance, practiced by both blacks and whites. It was not simply by chance that this crossing of boundaries occurred during the development of the civil rights movement.

The media and American mass culture exerted major influence on rock 'n' roll music and dance forms. A national explosion of rock 'n' roll occurred in movie houses, where Bill Haley and the Comets' rendition of "Rock Around the Clock" in the film *Blackboard Jungle* caused "riots."[15] But the exposure the music and dance received from television consolidated rock 'n' roll as a mass phenomenon: millions of people watched Elvis Presley's appearances (and later, those of the Beatles) on the "Ed Sullivan Show." Dick Clark's "American Bandstand," a daily television program in which Philadelphia teenagers danced to the latest hit records, provided teenagers a national forum for learning social dance in their own homes (see illustration 10).

"American Bandstand" was a particularly interesting phenomenon, a daily dance party placed in front of the television camera. The performers, ordinary high school students neither professionally trained nor specially selected, attended the show every day after school. The "regulars" became celebrities with whom the home viewers identified (Belz 1972:102–3). Dance in this case constituted both performance and be-

14. For an account of the history of vernacular dance, see Stearns and Stearns 1968.
15. According to Stearns and Stearns (1968:2), Haley's recording sold over three million copies, a large number at that time.

10. Two teenagers perform for their peers on the set of "American Bandstand."
The Bettmann Archive.

havior; dancers were everyday people, as involved with themselves and the others with whom they danced as with an audience. The union of performance and behavior in "American Bandstand," never an explicit artistic canon for the television program, became an idea which later surfaced in experimental dance of the '6os and in contact improvisation.

Rock 'n' roll signaled other changes in dance style related to the influence of both black dance traditions and the mass media. People tended to dance in less predetermined, partnered forms so that participants were more closely connected to a room full of people than to a single person of the opposite sex. At the same time, greater individual interpretation of the movement forms was also becoming permissible. Music critic Carl Belz suggests:

Each dancer became absorbed in a world of intense, personal experience. Visually, a rock dance provided the counterpart of the way rock music was otherwise most typically experienced—that is, by transistor radios which allowed a massive audience to share the

11. People dancing in the seats and aisles of the Paramount Theatre in New York during a rock 'n' roll show in 1957 seem to have a range of reactions. But the young man in the center appears quite self-absorbed in dancing alone to the music. The UPI caption for this photo claimed that "some five thousand teen-agers in sweaters and leather jackets blocked Times Square while waiting to get in. Today a large force of cops is on hand to prevent a repetition of yesterday's near-riot." UPI/Bettmann Newsphotos.

> same experience, but to feel it individually. The bond among the dancers resided in the music they heard, but their physical separation showed that the bond was privately felt. In the panorama of a rock dance, one could not determine who was dancing with whom; rather everyone seemed to dance with everyone else. (1972:91)

Thus improvisation allowed for highly individualized dancing, and at the same time that dancers became more individualized, they participated in a collective experience. In situations like rock concerts and dances, no one needed to have a date, no one needed to be asked to dance, and, at least in theory, no one needed to have learned the right steps.

By the mid-'6os, people in some communities had carried improvisational flexibility in rock 'n' roll dancing to the point at which it was

12. The danger of (white) teenagers driven out of control by rock 'n' roll music and dance figured prominently in press coverage of the period. This 1959 photograph of a London "ballroom" carried a UPI caption which discussed attempts to ban the American film "Rock Around the Clock" because "riots resulting in considerable damage have occurred in movie houses." However, in this photograph, no one in the sedate crowd seems close to being riotous; the freely flowing, ongoing quality of the movement and the internal focus of the young man are the most evident features. UPI/Bettmann Newsphotos.

acceptable for dancers simply to go out onto the dance floor, alone or with friends, and "get into" the music, moving in individual, idiosyncratic styles. But although the "steps" were not codified and most people felt they were being "free," certain structural and stylistic characteristics still typified the dancing. Dancers improvised, but did so within a specific movement range. They tended to move with a focus inward rather than outward to a partner or to the environment, absorbed by the music and the experience of moving. They frequently danced with a sense of freely sending energy in all directions, creating an impression of abandon and literally giving up control.

The movement qualities of rock dance created important components of the cultural environment of that time. Engaging in these ways of

13. The large crowd at a rock concert in Ione, California, in 1969 is typical
of gatherings at outdoor music festivals in the '60s. The UPI caption states
that "young nudes danced in a haze of marijuana smoke" but that "there were
no reported incidents beyond monumental traffic jams." This comment links
sex, drugs, and possible violence with rock music and dance. UPI/Bettmann
Newsphotos.

moving shaped peoples' feelings about their lives. The movement style
seemed natural, contemporary, open, and not "uptight." Along with the
rock music of the period, dancing both reinforced and crystalized an
image of the self:[16] independent yet communal, free, sensual, daring.
This image of self would be central to contact improvisation.

The movement qualities of rock dancing were also associated with
contemporary social movements and practices such as the civil rights
movement, youth culture, and drug-taking, and with values such as rebellion, expressiveness, and individualism within a loving community of
peers. Dancing encoded these ideas in a flexible and multilayered text,
its kinesthetic and structural characteristics laden with social implications
and associations. Depending on the circumstances and cultural back-

16. "In the last instance," write the editors of *The 60s Without Apology*, "it was the music
and the attached dance forms that really created a new public sphere, even more than the
various code violations in dress and speech" (Sayers et al. 1984:6).

grounds of the participants or observers, different aspects of the dancing would emerge as primary (see illustrations 14 and 15).[17]

For example, the twist, made popular (ca. 1961) by black musician/composer Chubby Checker, was at once perceived by segments of the (white) American public as overly sexual because of its pelvic movements and open derivation from black culture, and antisocial because of the separation of one dancer from another. In 1962, one English journalist visiting New York wrote:

> "I'm not easily shocked but the Twist shocked me . . . half Negroid, half Manhattan, and when you see it on its native heath, wholly frightening. . . . I can't believe that London will ever go to quite these extremes . . . the essence of the Twist, the curious perverted heart of it, is that you dance it alone." (Beverly Nichols quoted in Nik Cohn 1969:105.

To opponents of rock 'n' roll dancing, the twist appeared shockingly autoerotic. It blurred the distinction between male and female in an unhealthy way, promoted wildness, immorality, and social deviance, and contributed to a "generation gap." To those who danced the twist or enjoyed watching it, the movement engaged similar but more sanguine meanings—it was sexy, exciting, wild, youthful, and new. In any given social setting, meanings could shift. For instance, those who danced the twist in New York City's Peppermint Lounge experienced it as a symbol of the latest and the newest, an activity of belonging in a chic social circle. But for some teenagers, forbidden to do the dance in schools or community centers, it was an act of rebellion against repressive authority.

Dancers engaged in social action gave social significance to rock dancing throughout the '60s. For many members of the counterculture, the free-flowing, internally focused dancing evoked and accompanied the experience of giving up control and losing oneself in the drug experience. For more politically minded people, rock dance constituted a metaphor for political awareness. The extensive improvisation in rock dance enacted the rejection of explicit structures by New Left and feminist organizations. Being able to "do your own thing" on the dance floor

17. Sociologist and rock critic Simon Frith (1984) makes a similar point about the flexibility of music: "Music matters to 60s politics for its openness, its ambiguity. It was possible, for example, for some performers (the Doors, Jimi Hendrix, the Rolling Stones, the Grateful Dead) to be a source of solidarity and enthusiasm for both the antiwar movement and the American soldiers in Vietnam" (67–68).

14. Dance can take on different meanings in different circumstances. Compare this photograph of Pentecostals picketing a rock 'n' roll show at the Paramount Theatre in New York in 1957 with illustration 15. UPI/Bettmann Newsphotos.

15. Teenagers perform rock 'n' roll dance in the main aisle of the Old South Church in Boston during a "contemporary service" in 1968. UPI/Bettmann Newsphotos.

16. Chubby Checker, *center,* who popularized the twist, dances in a 1960 publicity photo with Conway Twitty, *left,* and "American Bandstand" emcee, Dick Clark, *right.* UPI/Bettmann Newsphotos.

enacted a commitment to individualism and egalitarian ideals frequently voiced in '60s politics by the New Left. The development of new music and dance forms by black artists continued an identification with and pride in black culture fostered in the civil rights and black liberation movements. And the lack of differentiation between male and female movement symbolized a rebellion against American gender roles.

As explicit political phenomena, the student movement, the civil rights and the black liberation movements, the antiwar movement, and the women's movement found only tenuous moments of alliance with each other. But dancing, a multivocal and flexible sphere of social activity, could on occasion alleviate and even transcend political differences, emphasizing the shared ethos of these movements for social change.

Experimental Dance and Theater in the '60s

The Judson Church Dance Theatre, a performance collective existing from 1961 to 1964, and the experimental or avant-garde modern dance

movement, of which it was the most publicized representative, also manifested and heralded social change. The temporary economic expansion
experienced during the '60s created conditions which allowed for the
simultaneous development of both formal and organizational possibilities
in dance. Experimentation with new ideas could be realized in a period of
relative economic ease; young dancers and students lived inexpensively
in cities like New York and San Francisco on the money brought in by
part-time work and helpful families.[18] Greater numbers of dancers were
able to band together to perform, and the number of aspiring choreographers increased dramatically. At the same time, choreographers found or
created more flexible circumstances in which to perform.[19] They began
to present work in more informal (and inexpensive) settings—churches
and loft spaces rather than concert halls.

Choreographers and dancers, sharing in the general social milieu of
incipient change and the specific representations of change in rock dance
and late-'50s modern dance, began to investigate ways to increase spontaneity, informality, and collective action in the production and performance of dance. The organization of the Judson Church group itself differed significantly from most dance organizations in the 1950s. From
1962 to 1964, the group presented sixteen concerts at the Greenwich
Village church at Washington Square. Anyone who wished to show a
piece could come to a meeting at which the program was collectively decided upon. More than forty artists, predominately choreographers but
also visual artists and musicians, showed their work during this period of
time, work wideranging in aesthetic precepts but often characterized by
experimentation with movement and new possibilities for structuring it.
Dancers investigated "everyday" movement, used improvisational and indeterminate structures, and borrowed ideas from sports, visual art, and
theater. They experimented with treating the body as a neutral enactor
of movement rather than as an expressive, gendered personality.[20]

In striking ways, the experimental theater dance was quite different

18. Yvonne Rainer, one of the most influential choreographers of her generation,
estimates that during her first two years in New York City her mother sent her ten thousand
dollars (1974:4).

19. This artistic trend had been initiated largely by visual artists in the '50s who began
organizing "happenings" in loft and warehouse spaces in New York. For an account of this
movement, see Kirby 1965.

20. In *Democracy's Body* (1984), Sally Banes describes in detail the concerts presented
from 1962 to 1964. Reviews of some of the Judson work by Jill Johnston, the *Village Voice*
journalist who first made the Judson Church Dance Theatre famous, can be found in *Marmalade Me* (1971). Also see Jowitt 1988, chapter 8, Kirby 1969, and Tomkins 1980 for
discussions of '60s theater dance.

17. Critic Jill Johnston described Steve Paxton's "Satisfyin' Lover" (1968) as "thirty-two any old wonderful people . . . [walking] across the gymnasium in their any old clothes. The fat, the skinny, the medium, the slouched and slumped, the straight and tall . . . that's you and me in all our ordinary everyday who cares postural splendor." (1971: 137). See Banes 1977: 71–74 for Paxton's score for the dance. Photo © 1968 by Peter Moore.

18. For a 1970 "flag show" at Judson Church "protesting arrests of people purportedly 'desecrating' the American flag" in demonstrations against the Vietnam War, Yvonne Rainer was asked to present a piece. "To combine the flag and nudity seemed a double-barreled attack on repression and censorship," wrote Rainer, *center,* whose dancers tied flags around their necks, removed their clothes, and performed "Trio A" (1974: 171–172). Photo © 1970 by Peter Moore.

19. The tasklike investigation of pedestrian actions which characterized one aspect of '60s experimentation was a major concept in Yvonne Rainer's "The Mind Is a Muscle," performed in this photo by Steve Paxton, David Gordon, and Yvonne Rainer (beginning the section called "Stairs"), and Becky Arnold (finishing the section called "Mat"). Photo © 1968 by Peter Moore.

20. Some experimental dance in the '60s drew directly on social dance forms. Xavier Nash, a member of the San Francisco Dancers' Workshop (directed by Anna Halprin), here leads a group of students in a "black dance soul train." Courtesy of Anna Halprin.

21. Audience members join in social dance on stage, displaying a wide range of movement styles, in a piece called "Sing-Along Sun King" (1970) by Richard Bull. Courtesy of Richard Bull.

from the social dance of the same time period. An obvious distinction is that rock 'n' roll dance and music were large-scale social activities, while theater dance was confined to a relatively small number of people clustered most noticeably in New York and other metropolitan and university centers. Most theater dancers participated in social dance, but only a handful of social dancers performed theater dance.

Contrasts in movement style also frequently existed. Rock dance tended toward exuberance and complex anarchy, while theater dance was often pedestrian and minimal. The familiar joke summarized the situation: in the early '6os, everyone would go to a dance concert to watch people stand around, and then afterwards everyone would go to a party and dance.

At the same time, a fusion of aesthetic and social ideas was occurring in theater dance. The aesthetic proposal that any movement could

be considered dance proved a powerful concept for younger dancers
engaged by ideals of social equality and community. These ideals were
embedded in the experience of social dance, which required no formal
training and was hence seen as "democratic," but which was also clearly
"dancing."

Thus, although the movement styles of experimental theater dance
and social dance often differed, a curious thematic unity existed between
them. Since the people doing both forms belonged to the same cultural
milieu (although that of social dance was much larger and broader),
the unity existing between the two dance genres came from a common
atmosphere of experimentation and adventure. Both contained an implicit message that what was being done had political meanings and was
making a statement.

Both social dance and theater dance of the '60s presented images of
gender roles which opposed mainstream images but did so in different
ways. Social dance was "oversexed" by public standards, its exuberance

22. The Performance Group, directed by Richard Schechner, warms up for
rehearsals of *Dionysus in '69*. Schechner explained to me that the warm-up
consisted of exercises designed to "give and get energy and motion from each
other." The man at the left performs a modified yoga pose ("We didn't know
then it was yoga"), and those in the center do a shoulder stand taught to the
group by Polish director Jerzy Grotowski. Also see Schechner 1973 (chapter 4).
Courtesy of the Richard Schechner Papers, Princeton University Library.

tied to "unnatural" sexual expression and its increasingly improvisational and individualistic structure tied to an attack on the proper partnership of a man leading a woman on the dance floor in recognizable patterns. Theater dance was often "undersexed" by public standards, androgynous, opposed to spectacular display of the body. Even though dancers might disrobe, nudity was seldom a sexual event but rather a presentation of some aspect of the physical body and its movement capacities, or a satiric commentary on itself or the subject matter of the dance.

The contrast of theatrical and social dance applies to only part of experimental performance, the part, in fact, with which Steve Paxton, the founder of contact improvisation, consciously allied himself. But Paxton and many other dancers also participated in and observed theatrical events that asserted the dramatic possibilities of the body.

"Physical theater" is a shorthand term for what were actually many kinds of experiments with generating theater that did not center on the text, but rather took the body and action as a starting point. Throughout America during the '6os an extraordinary amount of theatrical produc-

23. Anna Halprin, *at left*, assists students doing an "opening up" exercise with Jefry Chan at a workshop held on the outside deck of the Tamalpa Institute. For Halprin, "opening up" consisted of physical, mental, and emotional activity and interaction. Courtesy of Anna Halprin.

24. The choreographic nature of experimental theater is evident in this photograph of *Antigone* (1967) as performed by the Living Theatre (directed by Julian Beck and Judith Malina). The Living Theatre also experimented extensively with audience participation in plays like *Paradise Now* (1969), as did many theater groups at that time. Photo 1980 by Bernd Uhlig. Courtesy of Judith Malina.

25. The Performance Group preparing for the opening birth scene from *Dionysus in '69*, a performance that was as much like a dance as a play. Said Schechner, "The women stood, the men squatted, and everyone waited until the moment felt right to begin." Courtesy of the Richard Schechner Papers, Princeton University Library.

26. At the Esalen Institute, a center for gestalt psychology in California, instructor Bernard Gunther leads a class in body awareness in 1967. As in illustration 23, the class takes place out of doors, suggesting the assumed relationship between perception of body and a "natural" environment. UPI/ Bettmann Newsphotos.

tion occurred which emphasized an intense physicality, and which also took up some of the same issues as theater dance of the period: improvisation, social commentary, and crossing boundaries between performer and audience. The exuberance of social dance was easily matched by the emphasis on action and even physical risk-taking by groups such as the Living Theatre, the Open Theater, the San Francisco Mime Troupe, Bread and Puppet, and the Performance Group.[21] A significant number of contact improvisers received training in this kind of theater, a training which would contribute to one of the variations on contact improvisation.

Finally, interest in the experience and "truth" of the body also emerged in nontheatrical settings, in therapeutic developments which burgeoned in the '60s. Concern for movement training which was both

21. For a summary account of '60s theater, see Richard Schechner's (1982) "Homeric Lists" of collectives and performances and his discussion of the theatrical avant-garde. Inspiration for this theater also came from Europe, for example, from the writings of Antonin Artaud (1958) and from the work of the Polish director Jerzy Grotowski (1968). Grotowski described his "poor theatre" as one which needed no props, music, sets, or text, but only the actor, "a man who works in public with his body, offering it publicly." The actor achieves a "secular holiness" by casting off his everyday mask and allowing the deepest revelations of his body to emerge (33).

scientifically based and sensuously felt was manifest in the body work of F. M. Alexander (1969), Irmgard Bartenieff (1980), Lulu Sweigard (1974), and Moshe Feldenkrais (1972), and was implicit in gestalt and sensory awareness training centers like Esalen and the encounter-group movement (Egan 1971). Performers and teachers attempted to apply this basically therapeutic work to movement training, just as Erick Hawkins had used kinesiological ideas in his dance technique classes. People also investigated body training from other cultures, particularly the martial arts of China, Korea, and Japan—Tai Chi Chuan, karate, judo, and aikido—and also various forms of yoga and meditation from India.

Contact improvisation, to a remarkable degree, would manage to connect these different activities of social and theatrical dance, performance, and body work, combining them into a single form. It did so in several ways. The social structure of its practice and performance did not initially divide people into performers and students, professional dancers and social dancers. Everyone involved went to jams, practiced the dance form, and showed the dance form (or could potentially show it). Also, contact improvisation combined the sensuality of social dance with an objective stance towards the physical capacities of the body, an idea developed by experimental theater dance, and with a belief in the inherent truth and drama of the body, an idea prominent in physical theater. The qualities of free-flowing movement and focus on the inner experience of moving, so characteristic of social dance, were joined with interest in "natural" movement training, central to studies of body therapies and martial arts. These qualities became central features of the movement experience of contact improvisation.

Steve Paxton

As I have tried to suggest, the development of contact improvisation can be traced to many different sources. Certainly, the social and cultural circumstances existing through the '60s and in the early '70s made the dance form possible. But contact improvisation also resulted from specific ideas and movement practices of the '60s filtered through the particular sensibilities and talents of Steve Paxton, the man who is credited as being the initiator of contact improvisation. His ideas and actions were central not only to the formation of contact improvisation but also to the course of its development.

Steve Paxton was a gymnast who began dancing in high school in

Tucson, Arizona. Coming to New York in 1958, he studied and worked
with numerous people in dance, theater, and the visual arts. Paxton
turned twenty-one in 1960. When asked in 1983 what he saw as the major
concepts and people of the period which influenced and shaped his
own work, Paxton, who joined Merce Cunningham's company in 1961,
remembered being quite taken with Cunningham's assertion that any
movement could be dance and that any *body* could be viewed in some way
as "an aesthetic conveyor." Paxton recalled feeling that in the late '50s,
most dance companies seemed extremely uniform. The notion of physical beauty was very narrow, he thought, and in comparison, Cunningham's company appeared more varied. While Paxton felt Cunningham
never went as far as he might have with his investigation of movement or
of different physical types, his steps in that direction seemed significant
to Paxton.

Robert Ellis Dunn, a musical associate of Cunningham's and a colleague of Cage's, taught a dance composition class which became famous
as the meeting place and inspiration for many of the Judson Church
choreographers, of which Paxton was one. Dunn had worked with
Martha Graham and her musical director, Louis Horst and wanted to
devise a different way to teach composition which drew on the structures
and philosophical ideas of experimental music. Paxton felt that Dunn's
classes were "amazingly influential" for his own development of a performing aesthetic. Dunn often posed problems based on experiments
occurring in music; Dunn's presentation of chance procedures pioneered
in the work of John Cage provoked Paxton to search for ways "to make
movement arise," to derive it from a basis other than an established aesthetic or a traditionally trained body. Paxton explained:

> When you're a dancer, you can spend many hours a day dancing,
> working on your technique and following the aesthetic rules of
> whatever dances you're in, but there's still all the rest of the time.
> What is your body doing? How does it get you uptown to the class?
> You've got your mind on the rehearsal or some piece you're build-
> ing, but how do you manage to get uptown? How does it know to
> stick its hand in your pocket and get out the money and take you
> through the subway hassles? There's still an incredible reservoir
> of activity, quite separate from the technical activities that one is
> involved in as a dancer. To look at that was the aim. There was one
> other aim, which was to break down the hierarchy that seemed to

arise between people when one was a choreographer and one was
a dancer. . . . It seemed to me like social forms very much determined the look of dances, or were a strong factor in the way they
looked.

When asked what he meant by social forms determining the look of
dances, Paxton said that the usual choreographic process, at least at that
time, was "a dictatorship," a condition that affected not just the process
of making dances but the aesthetic and style of dances as well. "You
handed over your motive [for dancing] in those days to your teachers or
choreographers," he explained. "Your motive, your movement sources
were determined, controlled by them, and you struggled to be what they
were." To Paxton, dancers often ended up looking like neither themselves nor their teachers, but like "watered down versions" of their teachers. Thus, Paxton said, "I began looking for ways to initiate a dance and
cause movement to arise among people I was interested in seeing move
(in other words, I was making choices all along), but without me being
a figure whom they copied or who controlled them verbally or through
suggestion."[22]

In these brief comments, the beliefs held in common with Cunningham are evident. Paxton's reminiscence also makes clear the extent to
which interest during the '50s in phenomenology and Zen, opposition
to heroic events and traditionally symbolic vocabularies, and concern
for the pedestrian, the everyday, the "here and now," were given a new
political reading in the '60s.

Other artists in New York City influenced Paxton. He practiced theater improvisation with Eugene Lyons and watched the Living Theatre
work. He established close artistic and personal friendships with some
of Cunningham's associates, particularly Robert Rauschenberg, and with
artists in Robert Dunn's class and at Judson Church. Yvonne Rainer,
one of the most active and influential members of this latter group, performed often with Paxton and was sympathetic with his work. At a public
lecture in 1984, Rainer talked about some of the themes common to their
choreographic circle and about how she viewed Paxton's dances. She, like

22. In an interview with Sally Banes, Paxton expressed a similar interest in finding
out how movement could "arise": "'My feeling about making movement and subjecting it
to chance processes was that one further step was needed, which was to arrive at movement
by chance. That final choice, of making movement, always bothered my logic somehow. If
you had the chance process, why couldn't it be chance all the way?'" (Banes 1984:58).

Paxton, stressed the possibilities opened up by the conceptions of art put forward by Marcel Duchamp and John Cage: the theme of the everyday, the role of chance and indeterminacy, and the acceptance of any material as a possible vehicle for art.

Rainer perceived two currents of political meaning in the "Cage-Duchamp movement." The first derived from Zen and involved an acceptance of everything that happened. The second involved an "antigenius, antimasterpiece" attitude. On the one hand, Rainer said, the Cage-Duchamp movement fostered acceptance of "a fated, totally randomized order," and on the other hand, the movement fostered resistance to the status quo and "the way in which social structures are naturalized and promulgated." These two currents articulated by Rainer would be joined in contact improvisation, which seemed to encompass both attitudes toward the significance of events: allow the dance to happen and recognize that anybody can dance.

Rainer stressed the influence of feminist ideas on the transformation of dance in the period from the '50s through the '60s. She argued that the perceived sexual and social injustices existing in the culture at large in the '50s appeared in dance as well. If you wanted to be a choreographer and you were a woman, you became a modern dancer, for the more prestigious artistic role of ballet choreographer was reserved for men. Martha Graham, said Rainer, used to stress gender divisions between men and women in dancing; Graham also gave corrections in class that connected movement ability with sexuality ("if you accept yourself as a woman, your turnout"—outward leg rotation at the hip joint—"will increase").

Rainer saw a marked change in many dances of the early '60s in which men and women dancing did the same movements and were undifferentiated by gender. Rainer recalled Steve Paxton's dance "English," in which he tried to make everyone look more alike, even to the extent of using make-up to obliterate eyebrows and render features less distinct. She also described a dance by Trisha Brown, "Lightfall," performed by Brown and Paxton, who tried repeatedly to climb on and off each other's shoulders. Again, male and female differences were ignored (see illustrations 27 and 28).

Rainer admired Paxton's work, suggesting that Paxton's "stance as a dancer" was not really appreciated by many people at the time. He consistently refused to entertain the audience, she explained, often making dances which examined a narrowly defined area of movement and which

27 and 28. Trisha Brown and Steve Paxton in a sequence from Brown's "Light-fall" (1963). Rainer suggested that this piece "was an early version of contact improvisation, without the softness of the martial arts." Also see Banes 1984 (pp. 100–101) for another description of this dance. Photos © 1963 by Peter Moore.

were extremely minimal.[23] Rainer thought Paxton also sensed the implicit political statements behind movement: "He was very aware of the
importance of social content and attempted to integrate that into his
dancing."[24]

Paxton was one of the dancers with whom Rainer made "Continuous Project Altered Daily," an evolving piece which incorporated the
rehearsal process as part of the performance. "The whole world of spontaneous behavior on stage was opening up to us . . . we were interested in
unforeseen happenings, effort, spontaneous response," Rainer recalled.
That interest spurred the dancers in "Continuous Project" to begin to
perform as a collective improvisational group, the Grand Union, which
existed from 1970 to 1976.

For the six years that the collective performed in studios and at
colleges, the Grand Union practiced open-ended improvisation which
switched rapidly from surreal dramatic scenes to movement games to
personal, conversational encounter, all conceived of as being within a
context of extreme individual freedom for the performers (see illustration 29). As a member of this group, Paxton pursued his interests in
finding out how improvisation could facilitate physical interaction and
response and how it could allow people to "participate equally, without
employing arbitrary social hierarchies in the group" (Paxton 1971:130).
He was clearly concerned with developing new kinds of social organization for dance, noting in an article he wrote about the group:

> Many social forms were used during the 1960's to accomplish
> dance. In ballet, the traditional courtly hierarchy continued. In
> modern dance (Graham, Limon, Lang, et al.), the same social
> form was used except magicians rather than monarchs held sway.
> Post-modern dancers (Cunningham, Marsicano, Waring), main-
> tained alchemical dictatorships, turning ordinary materials into
> gold, but continuing to draw from classical and modern-classical
> sources of dance company organization. It was the star system. It

23. Jill Johnston (1971) described Paxton in 1968 as taking "the most extreme liberated positions. He likes people for what they are and believes in their physicality (their
shape and way of moving) for what it is" (97).

24. For descriptions of Paxton's dances and his commentary on choreography, see
Banes 1984 and 1987, and a videotaped interview with Steve Paxton by Nancy Stark Smith
("Steve Paxton: The Judson Project") at Bennington College in 1983. Also see Johnston
1971 and Rainer 1974.

29. The Grand Union performed a free-associative, anarchic kind of improvisational dance and theater, using dialogue, props, costumes, and music. In this photograph taken at a 1974 concert at Judson Church, Douglas Dunn reclines against Barbara Dilly, *foreground,* Steve Paxton and Trisha Brown clutch each other, *left,* while David Gordon, *back center,* looks on from a distance and Nancy Lewis, *center,* dances by herself. Photo © 1975 by Johan Elbers.

is difficult to make the general public understand other systems, inundated as we are with the exploitation of personality and appearance in every aspect of theatre. Though this basic poverty of understanding on the audiences' part is a drag, unique and personalized forms have been emerging, such as those seen in the works of Robert Wilson, Judith Dunn, Barbara Lloyd, and the Grand Union. (1971:131)

During this same period of time, Paxton studied the Japanese martial art form aikido and began to experiment with the rolling, falling, and partnering skills of that movement technique (see illustration 30). He played with the opposite experiences of extreme stillness and extreme

30. Annie Leonard throws her partner during her black belt examination in aikido. When Steve Paxton studied this form, he was impressed by the reflexive knowledge of the body invoked in the training and by what seemed to him to be an aesthetic based on physical necessity. Photo © 1989 by Jan Watson.

imbalance; "I wanted to launch myself off the planet and see what happened without having to worry about the re-entry a few seconds later," Paxton recalled. Moreover, Paxton was becoming interested in establishing a formal structure for improvisation rather than an anarchic one like that of the Grand Union, a structure (or antistructure) which Paxton thought was wonderful for "opening up all the possibilities" but which "eventually led to isolation of its members."

In January of 1972, Paxton taught the structure for an improvisational solo he had made for himself to a class of male students at Oberlin College. Paxton and eleven students performed the dance called "Magnesium" for an audience in a large gymnasium. A videotape taken by Steve Christiansen shows ten minutes of what was a slightly longer dance.[25]

The tape shows an event obviously set in the '60s (taken as a cultural period). The assorted loosely fitting pants and shirts and the long

25. My descriptions of videotapes here and in chapters 3 and 4 are based on a movement analysis carried out using the concepts of Rudolf Laban and of dance composition. See chapter 5 for further discussion and references.

hair provide obvious signs, but the quality of movement—the loose, awkward, wild abandon, the earnest directness—are immediately apprehended kinesthetic markers of this historical moment. Performing on several wrestling mats, the men stagger about, crash into each other, fall, roll, and get up only to lurch around again. A lot of hand-clasping and pulling or dragging occurs, so that the dance looks like drunken wrestling at times. The performers have no orientation toward the audience, pursuing their falling with a tasklike attitude.

The dancers generally use their bodies as one piece, all parts simultaneously thrust off balance or thrown against another body or into the air. They keep an inner-directed focus fairly consistently; sometimes focus moves to another dancer. Lack of control characterizes most movement as the body weight is pulled or thrown off balance, and the dancers passively fall against each other or to the floor. The falls look sudden and wild, although it is also evident that no one is getting hurt because of the mat and because the performers exercise some active control in softening or rolling as they hit the floor.

The lurching continues at a rapid pace for five minutes, then it slows. Several performers start to lift one man; the rest join in lifting this single person and lowering him slowly, upside down, until his head touches the mat. This event, and an earlier arm tugging duet, are the only encounters caught by the camera which last longer than about ten seconds. The falling then resumes, until Paxton begins what he has referred to as the stand, or the small dance, and the others join him (see illustration 31). Standing apart, facing different directions, the vertical quiet of the slightly swaying bodies contrasts sharply with the frenetic, off-balance motion which preceded it. After several minutes of the stand, the dancers walk off and the audience, which has responded audibly with applause and laughter throughout the dance, applauds again.

Contact improvisers cite "Magnesium" as the "seminal work" of contact improvisation, before the form was named, although Paxton and others had been experimenting with this kind of movement for some time.[26] Thus, 1972 became the year marking the start of contact improvisation. Ironically, that same year saw the demise of the antiwar move-

26. The naming of contact improvisation and the conception of it as a particular dance experiment are part of what made it seem unique. Many others in dance had experimented with both weight and improvisation, and throughout the '60s, examples abound of both specific dancers and dance and theater groups doing something akin to "contact improvisation," for example, Trisha Brown, Grand Union, Daniel Nagrin's Workgroup, Anna Halprin's San Francisco Dancers' Workshop, Julian Beck and Judith Malina's Living Theatre, and so on.

31. In "the stand," a meditative exercise to develop sensitivity to one's own weight and balance, people experiment with minimizing muscular tension and then noticing the subtle shifts of weight which result. This exercise constituted the final section of "Magnesium" (1972), Steve Paxton's piece, and was included in many subsequent contact improvisation showings. Courtesy of Daniel Lepkoff.

ment and, in retrospect, signaled the fading of the '60s as a distinctive political era.

Although Steve Paxton is acknowledged as the founder and original guide of the contact improvisation movement, it soon expanded and spread out beyond his direct control. As the social and political movements of the '60s faded and as even the social dancing of the '60s began to wane, people practicing contact improvisation perpetuated this period's values and characteristics, weaving them together into a unique artistic and social experiment in modern dance.

3

"You Come. We'll Show You What We Do"

The Initial Development of Contact Improvisation

In June 1972, several months after the performance of "Magnesium," Paxton received a two thousand dollar grant from Change, Inc., to perform at the John Weber Gallery in New York City. While touring with the improvisational dance collective the Grand Union, Paxton had met a number of students. He decided to invite somewhere between fifteen and twenty of them to live and work together for two weeks in exchange for room and board. Paxton also invited Grand Union colleague Barbara Dilley to join them, along with Mary Fulkerson, a teacher from the University of Rochester who had been working for some time with "release technique," a movement technique based on anatomical imagery and emphasizing softness and movement flow.[1] Among the students who would play a prominent role in the next few years were Nancy Stark Smith and Curt Siddall from Oberlin College, Danny Lepkoff and David Woodberry, both students of Mary Fulkerson's at the University of Rochester, and Nita Little, a Bennington College student. Steve Christiansen, a video artist who had wandered accidentally into the "Magnesium" performance at Oberlin and recorded it, also joined the group to videotape.

The group continued to work with Paxton's investigation of two ex-

---

1. Fulkerson's history includes sources described in the previous chapter and illustrates the variety of ways in which dance influence is transmitted. She studied with Anna Halprin in California, with Marsha Paludan (also a former student of Halprin's), who worked with a company of children and adults at the University of Kansas, and with Barbara Clark (1975), a New Mexico teacher who combined improvisation with kinesiological work based on Mabel Ellsworth Todd. Paludan later became involved in contact improvisation as well.

tremes of physical disorientation explored in "Magnesium," the one extreme of hurling oneself about and the other extreme of standing still
and noticing the tiniest impulses of movement in the body (what Paxton
had been calling the small dance, or the stand, for many years). Paxton
called the dancing contact improvisation, not because he thought it was
"the most poetic" name, but because, he said, "it accurately and objec-
tively described what we were doing."

Most of the dancers stayed in a Chinatown loft where they worked
on an Olympic-size wrestling mat, practicing aikido skills and testing the
possibilities of two bodies moving together while staying in physical contact. They also worked outdoors in New York City parks. Nancy Stark
Smith remembered that at the time it was "somewhat ambiguous" what
they were going to do together. The work sessions merged with living, so
that rehearsals never happened at set times but just went on "all day and
all night" throughout the ten days of preparation. Smith's description
immediately recalls themes of experimental dance—the interest in blurring distinctions between "art" and "life" and in replacing "goal-oriented"
dance with communal experimentation.

> We kind of lived in the midst of whatever it was that was begin-
> ning to take effect, because we spent so much of the day rolling
> around and being disoriented and touching each other and giving
> weight. . . . The fact that we weren't working towards anything,
> but just working, gave it a feeling of freedom to play with things.
> You weren't wondering whether you were doing it well or not,
> you were just doing it. . . . Everyone had a different way of doing
> it—the releasing people were very soft and light, very sensitive.
> The jocks, and I guess I was one of them, were out there rolling
> around and crashing about. . . . But we had to work together, or
> at least we did work together, even though people had favorite
> partners. . . . How to live together as a group and how to do this
> movement were equally new ideas to me.

The First Years

From the evidence provided by participants' descriptions and by videotape records of the dancing, contact improvisation at this time consisted
primarily of duet encounters in which one or both partners would jump
and fall, using the body of the other person as leverage to direct the fall.
Sometimes, one person would climb on another or would gently guide

a partner's movement by lightly touching him or her. The jumping and falling show the influence of aikido skills, the lighter touching gives evidence of the body awareness work of "the small dance" and also of the influence of Mary Fulkerson and her students.[2]

The videotape "Chute" consists of edited segments from over twenty hours of tape documentary of rehearsal for the John Weber Gallery Concerts in New York City, June 1972. A commentary by Steve Paxton was added to the ten-minute video, which Steve Christiansen originally taped and which Christiansen, Lisa Nelson, and Paxton edited in 1978. Fourteen dancers appear, male and female students and colleagues of Paxton working for the first time with contact improvisation.

The dancing in this tape consists of duets. Like "Magnesium," virtually all the encounters take dancers from standing down to the floor, as the dancers experiment with falling. They seem to be testing out and extending possibilities, so that the duets last much longer than a single fall and a roll. In contrast with the almost continuous, impulsive tumbling of "Magnesium," dancers lean and balance on each other in a sustained, suspended manner, fall off and jump back onto each other, and trade the role of supporting or being supported several times in the course of a duet encounter. A greater sense of relationship between the dancers also appears, usually playful and tender, so that the action is less tasklike and more partner-oriented than in "Magnesium."

Again, the dancers often use the body in a whole piece, but sometimes parts of the body are articulated through successive movements— one body part moving after another—particularly in the rolling actions. Body parts are also used on the floor as support for the whole body— not only the torso and feet, as in "Magnesium," but also the shoulder and head, hips, and hands. Individual dancers also use the bodies of other dancers as supports, and moments of balance of one body on top of another occur. Some of the partnering interactions which eventually became part of the technique of the form appear: curving over a partner's back, catching a partner hip to hip, one person rolling perpendicularly over another on the floor ("surfing").

In "Chute" as in "Magnesium," the dancers concentrate on internally sensing movement rather than intentionally placing their bodies

2. Danny Lepkoff remembered that the Chinatown loft "was a massage hospital after every performance," but that he and the other Rochester people seldom became sore or bruised because they had learned how to fall softly. David Woodberry suggested that Fulkerson's releasing work had a strong effect on the subsequent development of contact improvisation.

in particular shapes or paths in space. However, the spatial pathways through which the bodies fall and the movement qualities displayed differ somewhat from those in "Magnesium." Because bodies are actually being used as supports and as moving entities which can break or guide another body's fall, the patterns in space outlined by the body as it moves (what movement theoretician Rudolf Laban called the trace-forms of movement) often spiral through three dimensions. Contact improvisers talk about having to acquire a "spherical" sense of space, with which they attempt, as Paxton says in his commentary for this videotape, to transform "vertical momentum into horizontal travel."

As the dancers attempt to extend the duet encounter, movement phrases lengthen and the quality of movement extends beyond passive free falling. At times, dancers control the movement in order to guide the momentum of an encounter or keep it going. They also direct their movements with intentional strength or lightness in order to guide a fall. Consequently, in general, the dancing in "Chute" has a greater visual variety than in "Magnesium," with qualities of freely flowing energy and passive weight still predominating.

The preparation and performances at the John Weber Gallery gave the blueprint for concerts to come in the next few years. The performances themselves constituted a continuation of the rehearsals, lasting five hours each day; the audience came and stayed as long as desired. There were no special lighting effects, costumes, music, or sets, only the wrestling mat which was occasionally moved aside so that the dancers did not have to confine themselves to such a small space. The plans for performing (like the plans for rehearsing and plans for the future) remained indefinite.

At the same time, Paxton and some of the other dancers began to take steps to have the work continue. In Amherst, Massachusetts, at the end of the summer of 1972, Curt Siddall arranged a reunion of the Weber group, along with new people who had learned contact improvisation from original group members. Paxton, a relatively well-known dancer now because of his work with Cunningham, Judson Church, and the Grand Union, was often invited to perform at colleges, galleries, and in small performance spaces. He started taking some of the John Weber dancers with him to show what they had been working on together.

In January 1973, Little, Siddall, Smith, Paxton, and Karen Radler (a Bennington student), plus Steve Christiansen (the video artist who had also by this time begun to dance), toured the West Coast, calling their event "You come. We'll show you what we do," an apt expression of the

demonstrationlike, experimental character of these performance showings. The following summer, Paxton took Smith, Lepkoff, and Annette
LaRoque, another Bennington student, to Rome, Italy, where, joined
by Mary Fulkerson, David Woodberry, and several other dancers, they
performed a series of concerts at the L'Attico Gallery.

The videotape entitled "Soft Pallet," shot by Steve Christiansen and
edited by him and Lisa Nelson, excerpts sections from the L'Attico Gallery performances. The loose clothing worn by the dancers and the use
of a mat are the same as in "Magnesium" and "Chute," but the dancers'
conception of contact improvisation has changed during the intervening
year. Dancers extend individual phrases of movement and connect one
to the other, forming long, continuous sequences lasting thirty seconds
or more. The duets often seem to take on an overall quality or theme.
Paxton and Woodberry do a quick, high-energy dance moving suddenly
together and apart. Fulkerson and Smith softly roll and balance, dancing fluidly and almost cradling each other. In another sequence, Paxton
manuevers and carries Lepkoff for some time; finally the balance is reversed and Lepkoff lifts Paxton.

The body articulation has become more extensive in this performance. Bodies twist and slither as if segmented into a number of parts
as frequently as they move all in one piece, and the number of ways in
which the dancers mutually support weight has increased. As a result of
a greater technical ability to fall and to catch weight, the dancers take
risks, launching themselves into space and moving through space in many
different patterns, usually curved and spiraling in nature. In one aston-
ishing moment in this improvisation, David Woodberry suddenly jumps
high into the air, feet tucked under him in a squatting position. Paxton,
standing to the side of Woodberry and apparently using his peripheral
vision, thrusts his arm out and hooks Woodberry under his knees. Woodberry falls backwards, dangling completely upside-down from Paxton's
arm, and Paxton slowly lowers him to the floor. The jump, catch, and fall
happen in about two seconds' time.

The dancing in these sequences feels unrelenting in its concentration and energy, filled with jostling, pushing, and pulling as well as with
gentler yielding, falling, and rolling.[3] A certain amount of crashing and

3. To some extent, the high energy which characterizes the "Soft Pallet" videotape
results from editing decisions. There were also many long, slow contact duets in this early
dancing. Judging by the short excerpt from such a duet visible in this tape, the slow dancing
shared with the faster duets an intense, absorbed, inward quality, the two dancers seeming
completely engaged in their encounter and oblivious to anything around them.

sudden falling still exists, making the mat look necessary and giving some of this dancing a rough and precarious appearance. Yet other sections display a technical skill in extended periods of supporting and balancing and in sometimes breath-taking falling and rolling.

The videotape includes one solo. Annette LaRoque rolls and falls, shifting support from one body part to another using predominately freely flowing movement and passive weight, with occasional sudden changes of direction. She seems completely involved in the internal sensation of movement. The solo indicates the development of a certain style which characterizes contact improvisation, a movement style which derives from duet and group interaction but which can be extrapolated and performed by a dancer alone.

For these performances, the dancers constructed a mat, but they were finding it increasingly impractical to rely on having a mat for every performance. The subsequent absence of cushioning would affect the style of the dancing, encouraging the synthesis of the gymnastic/aikido skills with a more ongoing and controlled flow of movement and with lightness of touch.

Throughout this early period, according to Nancy Stark Smith, Paxton set a mood of "directness, simplicity, and lack of context," a mood "probably affected by the people he was working with but still largely attributable to him." In the early years, the contact improvisers often said that contact improvisation had no aesthetic. Of course, Smith added, when you look at it and compare it with other dance forms, you see that it does have a particular aesthetic.

> But we were working from the inside of it, not working relative to anything else. The focus was on sensation, not particularly on style, on psychology, on aesthetics, on theater, on emotions. It was really pared down so that we could deepen our practice of the physical aspects of the work, so that we could find out what was possible instead of what looked nice.

Judging by comments from Smith and other dancers, participants took the focus on physical aspects as a neutral value, a part of natural law rather than an aesthetic (cultural) overlay.

Paxton expressed the same idea in a slightly different way, saying that contact improvisation excited him because it could be taught, at least initially, "so much faster than regular dance material where long, slow changes are required in the muscles to meet an aesthetic ideal." Quickness in learning implied an accessibility absent from virtuoso modern dancing and ballet. In contact improvisation, according to Paxton, the aesthetic ideal might be said to be "a totally integrated body" (McDermott 1977:6).

Between the times of performance showings during these first two years, dancers living in different places might have communicated seldom or not at all. However, those individuals who wanted to continue investigating and practicing contact improvisation began to teach what they knew to other people in order to have partners with whom to dance. Contact improvisers take pride in the process of "passing the dance on," seeing this process as part of the "folk" nature of the form and as a demonstration of how the form itself requires that the dance be shared. A favorite analogy, told to me by many different people and attributed originally to Christina Svane, is that of contact improvisation to poker. "When a poker player goes to a new town and no one knows how to play, he has to teach someone in order to have a game."

Performances, Audiences, and New Dancers

From 1973 to 1975, the number of people doing contact improvisation increased rapidly. The students who had studied with Paxton at Oberlin

32. Steve Paxton and Nita Little. Photo © 1975 by Edmund Shea.

and Bennington graduated from college and began to resettle in other places; in particular, Curt Siddall, Nancy Stark Smith, and Nita Little, who all moved to California, taught and practiced contact improvisation regularly, always in informal settings. Alan Ptashek, who lived in a communal house with Nancy Stark Smith, said her classes were set up very casually, in large part just for the people in the house who constituted "three-quarters of her class." Ptashek added, "One of the unique things to me in my orientation to contact was practicing it with the people I lived with. That described contact to me in a very immediate way."

Performance opportunities at colleges, galleries, and experimental theaters continued to arise for the contact improvisers as a result of Paxton's reputation, which drew invitations to perform, or, increasingly, because one of the other dancers would set up a showing or because an enthusiastic viewer wanted to arrange a performance. Lisa Nelson, who began performing contact improvisation in 1975, recalled that the concerts would "come together very quickly"; the people who were to participate would gather just before the concert or, sometimes, not until the concert began.

> There was always someone new to dance with in a concert—that I
> remember clearly. . . . I remember a tremendous tension and ex-
> citement about encountering anybody, an anticipation, not know-

33. Nancy Stark Smith and Nita Little. Photo © 1976 by Uldis Ohaks.

ing what was going to happen—whether you were going to dance slowly, hardly move, do a lot of lifting and falling, or whether it was going to be sensuous or kind of playful or combative.

The ambiance of unpredictability, of exhibiting behavior as a process rather than presenting something as a finished product, resided within a loose structure, the "round robin," which participants adopted as a convention. A round robin starts with two people dancing. Then either one leaves the other to solo until joined by a new partner, or a third person interrupts the duet to form a new pair, and so on (sometimes three or more people dance together). Although it is never specified or required, those who have already danced often wait until most others have a turn before reentering the action.

Lisa Nelson's description of early performances points to the dancers' characteristic sense of being engaged in a process:

> The performances were like a demonstration. It was very rough and you could drop in and out and it was okay. . . . Duets would last ten or fifteen minutes, sometimes even twenty. The solo work in between was more episodic, usually very weight-oriented, jumping and falling, and falling and rolling. . . . When everyone had a chance to dance with as many people as possible, it would be over. As a person in the audience, and as a learning performer, you really got to see how the different levels would occur, starting from the more tentative contact, perhaps, to a real physical contact, bumping up against each other, to some very poignant, very soft communicative duet . . . there was a sense of danger in it, always.

The physical risks of failing while supporting or being supported by another person, depending on the other's response as well as one's own reflexes to help guide the fall, were at their greatest in these early years when the skills had not been completely developed and when people were constantly testing what might be done.

Through these performances or showings, an audience for contact improvisation began to develop. Students, dancers, and a more general population interested in experimental art and dance came to see the work. Some of the people who performed during those first three or four years gave descriptions of performances and of the responses by the audience, which point to the peculiar way in which contact improvisation mingled dance with sport and art with socializing:

> The performances were so exciting, and it thrilled me to be in them. . . . I always felt there was a gut-level response from the audience about what they were seeing. You understand that this is just my impression, but the response—the applause, the "oohs" and "aahs," the laughter—was just a real physical response. It was almost like seeing a hot basketball game. (Danny Lepkoff)

> The first tour of the West Coast was called "You come. We'll show you what we do." And that was really the attitude, a kind of welcoming of people to come in and see what we were up to. . . . Some of my favorite performances were in the early years, because people hadn't seen anything like this before, and they weren't jaded or glib about it. When they'd see somebody falling, they'd gasp because they weren't used to seeing that be anything other than a terrible accident.

> What happened, I think, was that sensations were transmitted to the audience. They would come out of the performances flushed and sweating, almost, and thrilled as if they had been doing it themselves. . . . To tell you the truth, I don't think there was one performance we did that wasn't very enthusiastically received. It was like we had offered something to people as a way of looking at movement and a way of experiencing movement that was very new and healthy, very vital and life-supporting. And it was very refreshing to people, I think. (Nancy Stark Smith)

> I always remember the same response, basically. The space would get warmer and warmer throughout the performance, and when it was over, there would be a lot of dancing in the audience. People would be jumping all over one another. They would stick around afterwards and really want to start rolling around and want to jump on you. The feeling was of a real shared experience among performers and audience, a tremendous feeling of physical accessibility between performers and audience. People would embrace you after a performance to congratulate you, but then they'd hang on you, lean on you.

> I think that looking at weight and seeing how long it was possible to touch somebody and not come away was very infectious.

34. Nancy Stark Smith and Curt Siddall. Photo © 1976 by Ted Pushinsky.

> . . . It was a very, very impressive postperformance state, extremely
> energized. There was something that really unified everybody.
> (Lisa Nelson)

A dynamic of interaction and sense of group participation characterized these early events, a dynamic generated by the movement style itself
(athleticism, risk-taking, extensive touching), the novelty of the dance
form, the informal nature of the performances, and the sensibility of
the audiences who saw them. The ambiance of the initial years of contact improvisation (1972–76) contrasts with the ambiance ten years later,
when the dynamic was clearly altered by changes in the dance form, the
dancers, and the audience's sensibility.

Among those who saw the early contact improvisation concerts were
people who subsequently sought out places to learn how to do it. The
geographical mobility of young people at the time, coupled with the experimental spirit which carried over from the '60s, made it possible for
contact improvisation to begin spreading across the country. The concise
nature of the dance form itself, the clear focus on maintaining physical
contact within an improvisational structure of falling off balance, also
made rapid transmission possible. Moreover, in contrast to all traditional

modern dance techniques, contact improvisation had no set vocabulary to learn; one could begin to practice it almost immediately, moving individually however one already moved.

Contact improvisation, because of its basis in physical notions of internally sensing weight and touch, rather than in a traditional aesthetic code, attracted both "dancers" and "nondancers." It drew people oriented towards performing who sought a new approach and people oriented towards recreational and therapeutic participation. Both the performing and the rehearsing/teaching ambiance of contact improvisation encouraged a sense of commitment on the part of each individual to a collective endeavor and, at the same time, encouraged conceptions of that endeavor as totally unstructured beyond the dance form itself. Even the restrictions of the dance form, the actions of giving and taking weight in contact with one or more people, were generally characterized as being completely open-ended, allowing for individuality and freedom. While the definition of contact improvisation restricted it, helping to identify and clarify it, the thrust of its conceptualization, its ideology, characterized contact improvisation as open and "free," an experiment in movement research continuing the work of the '60s avant-garde.

Looking at just a few examples of individual experiences in those early years conveys a sense of the spirit and the process of developing contact improvisation. In 1972, Lois Welk and two of her college friends, Jill Becker and Donna Joseph (Chinabear), went to California. All three of them were interested in choreography and improvisation, and they formed a dance collective with some people they met in San Francisco, calling themselves the American Dance Asylum.

"You come. We'll show you what we do" arrived at the Fireside Theater that January (1973), and Welk compared her experience of seeing contact improvisation for the first time with the first time she saw modern dance: "My head was in a spin—it was so incredibly exciting." The "high physical level, the diving through space, were amazing," she remembered. "I was so impressed by their courage to go out and improvise for three and a half hours, their confidence in their partners and the group, the sense of relaxation about it all."

Welk and her friend Jill Becker talked to Paxton after the concert, who gave them permission to "crash" his class at Bennington College in Vermont.[4] The two women hitchhiked to Vancouver from San Francisco,

4. Paxton's Bennington class was taught outside of the regular curriculum. Paxton explained that, at the time, he was concerned about having genuinely serious students with

took the train across Canada, and camped out at Lisa Nelson's house, which was "like Grand Central Station." By July, Welk remembered, "I was out of my mind on contact improvisation."

Getting permission to offer a workshop in the Dance Department at the State University of New York–Brockport, her alma mater, Welk began to teach twelve students. Most of them became frightened at what they perceived as the potential physical danger.[5] By the end of the workshop, only two students remained, Arnie Zane, for whom this class was his first dance class,[6] and Bill T. Jones. Within a year, Welk, Zane, and Jones had settled in Binghamton, New York, to work together as the American Dance Asylum, teaching and performing for the next six years and supporting themselves on part-time jobs, teaching, and small grants. Both Welk and Jones experimented to find ways to integrate contact improvisation with other kinds of set and improvisational choreography, and Welk continued to teach contact improvisation for several more years at Binghamton.

In another part of the country, Dena Davida, a dancer who had learned ballet and gymnastics as a child and modern dance in college, was studying in Minneapolis, and teaching creative dance to children in 1974. Davida, influenced by learning about Laban movement analysis and the Moshe Feldenkrais system of body therapy, was looking for a way of moving that was "easeful" and not about "pushing and forcing." "Something felt wrong to me about traditional modern dance studies," said Davida, "about locking my hips in place as a way of 'centering' my body. I decided dance wasn't about struggling, but about moving."

Davida studied with Mary Cerney, a Minneapolis dancer with the Nancy Hauser Dance Company who had gone to California and learned contact improvisation from Nita Little.[7] When Cerney returned to Minneapolis, she began to teach contact improvisation. The "sensuality, weight, and flow" of contact improvisation made Davida feel like she had found

whom to work. Teaching the class outside of the curriculum required people to come to it out of interest and commitment, not because they were getting college credit.

5. Contact improvisation as Welk had learned it from Paxton in the spring was taught largely by simply practicing it, with a few preparatory exercises for warming up.

6. Arnie Zane later wrote that he "had always loved the reality of social dancing and junior high school parties," so he decided to try this workshop which was advertised as similar to social dance. "It was like taking acid; on a physical level, it was a total liberating experience in the early seventies" (in Kreemer 1987:113).

7. Little was one of the original Weber dancers. Contact improvisers in the '70s were usually familiar with the "lineage" of their teachers, tracing ancestry back to one of the original John Weber dancers.

35. Steve Paxton, *above,* and Curt Siddall. Photo © 1976 by Uldis Ohaks.

36. Nancy Stark Smith and Nita Little. Photo © 1976 by Rhoda Elend.

her "own medium." She remembered dancers considering the question of whether it was dance or not, of whether you wanted to watch it or not. Some were suspicious and saw contact improvisation as "mystical, cultlike" because, in fact, contact improvisers "did get pretty fanatical. People were infatuated with it, had to do it every day." Three years later, Davida moved to Montreal, where she became one of the major contact improvisation teachers and performers in that city.

These two examples of individuals who became involved with contact improvisation are typical in their indication that the dance form struck a strong, responsive chord within a particular segment of the American population in the early '70s.

Organization and the *Contact Quarterly*

The 1973 West Coast Touring Group (Little, Smith, Siddall, Radler, and Paxton) met again in California in 1975 (minus Radler, plus David Woodberry), calling themselves ReUnion, a name evoking both past social experience of dancing together and the nature of the dancing itself. The dancers exchanged teaching ideas and discussed experiences in addition to dancing and performing together. This exchange, and others like it, contributed significantly to the evolution of contact improvisation into a recognizable dance form. With time, certain teaching exercises occurred repeatedly, becoming recognized and defined,[8] and as more performances were given, more people identified both a movement style and a group of performers with the name contact improvisation.

The video camera also played a crucial role in developing contact improvisation. It provided constant feedback to dancers, showing them what the dancing that they were sensing internally looked like for an observer. Videotapes contributed to development of a shared movement vocabulary within an improvisational structure:

> When we'd watch the videotapes and see some outrageous things happen, there was a tremendous appreciation for that. Or we'd see a duet where a very complex thing had gone down, and we would see how they'd worked themselves out of it or into it. Maybe, because you had seen something on tape, or live, you would try

8. Teaching techniques were also willingly shared with other teachers. Participants agree that there was and is no sense of possessiveness about techniques or even a need to identify who created them.

> it. If it worked consistently, it might become vocabulary—certain throws, for example. These things were never taught as set "moves," but they appeared regularly. (Nancy Stark Smith)

The video camera became a kind of teacher, a means by which new movement and shared aesthetic values could be implicitly delineated.

The passage of time also began to make the ReUnion people feel that they were engaged together in more than a temporary enterprise. By the time they met in 1975, they were beginning to talk about formalizing their organization. Some of the dancers said they were also provoked by a growing worry about dangerous teaching and a sense of possible fragmentation and loss of reputation resulting from the uncontrolled spread of contact improvisation.

From the beginning, Paxton had been extremely concerned with "controlling the teaching of going out of control" so that participants would be safe from injury. Now, teachers whom the contact improvisers had never heard of were giving classes in what was called contact improvisation, and reports were coming in of students with sprains, joint

37. Steve Paxton and Nancy Stark Smith. Photo © 1976 by Ted Pushinsky.

38. Steve Paxton and Nancy Stark Smith. Photo © 1976 by Ted Pushinsky.

injuries, and stitches. Moreover, when the name started appearing in contexts that the originators did not recognize, they were concerned about what kinds of activity were being called contact improvisation.

At this critical juncture, a key development and counterdevelopment occurred. William Schrievogel, a writer who called himself Koriel and who lived in the same house with some of the contact improvisers, attended a meeting of the ReUnion group. He offered to act as a kind of manager for contact improvisation, helping to organize activities and protect the name.

In a photocopied newsletter sent out in 1975 by the ReUnion group and their friends from San Francisco, Koriel summarized a series of proposals, including stipulations that members of "the Company" (the ReUnion group) communicate monthly through Koriel, that members give over 10 percent of their net earnings to "the Contact Fund," that a "recognized teacher/performer of contact improvisation must be OK'd by two or more of the members of the Company . . . and must give over 5% of contact net earnings to the Contact Fund," and that recognized teacher/performers would be expected to communicate regularly.

The newsletter also included a proposal from Nita Little. She suggested that the company adopt the name Contact Core. She also reported that a friend of hers involved in arts management had suggested they start using "© Steve Paxton et al." whenever they used the words "contact improvisation" in publicity statements (*Contact Newsletter* 1[April 1975]).

These organizational proposals were never acted upon. Ideologically, the proposals seemed "not in the spirit" of contact improvisation, said one dancer, and in practice, no one wanted to sign the letters of agreement to trademark the name, an act which would have required regularly reporting activities and "policing" new teachers. When Koriel complained that no one was giving him any work, Steve Paxton suggested to him that maybe "it's just a really small job."

In November 1975, Nancy Stark Smith published a second newsletter at Stinson Beach, California. In it, she reported that the "core group" had decided to disband as a committee and discontinue having a manager. "Instead of being policemen, we have decided to put our energies behind fostering communication between all those doing contact and encourage those less experienced to continue working out but hold off teaching for a while." She added, "It feels a lot better this way" (*Contact Newsletter* 1[November 1975]).

Thus the first-generation contact improvisers moved in the direction of consolidating into a dance company and a school but quickly chose to avoid establishing a formal organizational structure and becoming involved in directly regulating procedures. They maintained a strong sense that what they were doing was ad hoc and spontaneous, both as dance and as social interaction, establishing these qualities as the hallmark of the form. They indirectly and informally handled the need for controls over the teaching of the material by continuing the newsletter and, in 1976, turning it into a magazine, the *Contact Quarterly*.

In fact, from the beginning, Steve Paxton and other involved dancers used the newsletter to articulate their ideas to others and exercise informal leadership. Paxton in particular strongly argued that the original precepts of the form be explored fully before being expanded to include other ideas. For example, the first newsletter (April 1975) includes a letter from Paxton describing his classes and reaffirming his approach to the work, ending with a comment on his dissatisfaction with dancers wanting to move in other, more metaphysical, directions.

> I want to go on record as being *pro-physical-sensation* in the teaching of this material. The symbolism, mysticism, psychology,

spiritualism are horse-drivel. In actually teaching the *stand* or
discussing *momentum* or *gravity,* I think each teacher should stick
to *sens*ational facts. . . . Personally I think we should guard our
thoughts about auras and energyfields and E.S.P. until we can
actually demonstrate *and* teach such matters. *Personally,* I've never
seen anything occur which was abnormal, para-physical, or extra-
sensory. Personally I think we underestimate the extent of the
"real." (Emphasis in original)

In a later issue of the *Contact Newsletter* (1[Summer 1976]), Paxton argued
in a slightly less vehement manner against the inclusion of overtly dramatic, emotional material in contact improvisation (a popular practice
in California, where people with theater background were beginning to
practice contact improvisation). Part of Paxton's emphasis on the physical
as reality and on physics as a natural phenomenon undoubtedly derived
from his effort to prevent contact from being turned into a vehicle for
psychic investigations or encounter therapy. At the same time, Paxton's
orientation towards the physical was not just oppositional; it constituted
a positive commitment with roots in the philosophy of '60s experimental
dance and in part of the modern dance tradition.

It seems clear that Steve Paxton, through his prestige as the movement's founder, his activity as a touring teacher and performer, and his
regular commentaries in the newsletter, exerted a considerable influence
on the development of contact improvisation in the first five years. As
people expanded the newsletter into the *Contact Quarterly*, voices other
than Paxton's became influential.

Furthermore, the establishment of the *Contact Quarterly* had a trans-
forming impact on contact improvisation and made it unique among
American dance techniques. Whereas the identities of other techniques
were consolidated through the formation of dance companies led by
founding choreographers and through the production of choreographed
works, contact improvisation was consolidated through the spread of the
practice of the dance form in collective groups and through the production of writing about it. During this period, at least, contact improvisation was an example of an alternative structure for organizing dance in
America.

The *Contact Quarterly* successfully provided a vehicle for promoting
and holding together a social network across the country and a forum
for discussing people's activities and ideas about contact improvisation. It
came to verify the existence of a movement; for the first time, as contact

39. David Woodberry, *above*, and Steve Paxton. Photo © 1976 by Uldis Ohaks.

improvisation spread to more people than could know each personally, participants began to talk about a "contact community" and a "contact network."

As pockets of contact improvisation activity sprang up across the country, local and regional versions and approaches to contact improvisation began to develop. New teachers and performers became leaders in their cities. Collectives organized to teach and explore the form. The contact jam became popular as a weekly local event in many places. Performing groups arose, some doing "pure" contact improvisation, others using the dance form in more dramatic or choreographic ways. Some of these groups were ad hoc, some of them incorporated as companies. New ideas were then disseminated through the *Contact Quarterly*. Because the dancing was based on principles of movement which were not attached to specific sequences or set technical exercises, a written vehicle could serve as a powerful educating and unifying force that augmented local developments.

By now, contact improvisation constituted a new dance form. It was new because it did not look like any other technique, and it was new because, despite Paxton's strong informal influence, it was not "Paxton technique." Unlike modern dance, which splintered into movement techniques with individuals' names attached (Graham, Humphrey-Weidman, Holm), contact improvisation remained a generic form.

4
Dance as "Art-Sport"
Continuing the Form

Although "Magnesium" heralded the beginning of contact improvisation, no one dance or event marked its coming of age. By the late '70s, however, groups all over the country were practicing the form, often in local variations influenced by the particular people involved. A videotape made by Stephen Petronio of a performance in Northampton, Massachusetts, in April of 1978, demonstrates the general qualities of contact improvisation at this time as well as indicating the particular contact style of the individual dancers: Andrew Harwood, Stephen Petegorsky, Lisa Nelson, Eleanor Huston, and Danny Lepkoff. In comparison with the videotapes from the early '70s, the dancing indicates a refinement and extension of technical skills accompanied by a slightly more presentational aesthetic. The videotape offers an image of contact improvisation six years after its inception.

A Performance in 1978

The performance at Northampton is a continuous dance, with choreographic conventions evident for entering the space. Sometimes dancers enter replicating the movement of someone already dancing. Sometimes, a solo dance serves as an entrance, a more complicated and extended version of the rolling, falling, shifting style seen in the solo in "Soft Pallet." Extensive trio work also occurs; the three men improvise an energetic sequence of jumping and tumbling over each other, interrupted by sudden stillnesses with one person at least partly balanced on another.

As in "Soft Pallet," bodies sometimes move compactly, all at once, and at other times move in smooth sequential segments, especially in slow, partnered rolls. But unlike "Soft Pallet," a sense of deliberately taking one's time and a degree of control over the flow of movement characterize a great deal of the dancing.

The uncontrolled abandon of the dancing seen in the early '70s has lessened in this Northampton performance. The dancers have mastered the use of certain tumbling skills (handstands, slow forward and backward somersaults, and aikido rolls) in conjunction with interaction in contact. They are able to play easily with one body draping or falling over the back of another, balancing there, and then controlling the fall to the floor, landing on either the hands or the feet. Dancers thus direct their weight actively instead of passively, sense the space all around them, and reach or carve their bodies out into the space, although passive weight and the amoebalike, internally sensed movement still play a large part in the dancing.

The major change lies in the general appearance of this performance as continuous dancing which is not entirely tasklike or focused solely on dancers' encounters with each other. Whereas "Soft Pallet" is exhaustingly energetic, even obsessive, in its pursuit of contact, the Northampton performance looks tamer by comparison, more measured, filled with more obviously conscious pauses, intentionally sustained sections, and the savoring of a still position or gesture—a kind of choreographic awareness. Movement occurs outside of the contact improvisation duet which is gestural or which consciously continues a movement idea as a theme, thus shaping the sequences in dancelike, or choreographic, ways. Perhaps because the action is slowed down, the dancers also seem more aware of the audience, not overtly, but in the absence of breaks in the flow of action and in the outwardly directed alertness of the dancers. People have acquired certain skills and a different sensibility, which have altered the relationship between performer and audience.

Expansion

During the mid- to late '70s contact improvisation underwent substantial changes as a result of increasing numbers of participants. Originally, the group of people doing contact improvisation had been "like a family," in which everyone knew everyone else and had shared many of the same experiences. People recruited close friends and lovers to the dance form,

so that dancing kinship was mixed with "real-life" kinship and friend-
ship. By the spring of 1976, the newsletter listed twenty-nine "Contacts,"
people actively teaching, performing, and/or organizing jams. By the following winter, forty-one individuals or groups were listed, each listing
often representing local complexes of contact improvisers. The "family"
was becoming greatly extended to include several hundred activists and
many more students who took contact improvisation classes.

These local groups developed around active teachers and performers, who formed the focal points and inspiration for their geographical
areas. Each local group helped to extend the dancing in a slightly different direction, in many cases developing a recognizable style of doing
contact improvisation. The largest general difference in styles developed
between the two coasts: the East Coast became known as the center of the
"pure" contact improvisers, followers of the form unembellished by any
theatrical elements;[1] the West Coast, particularly California (except for
ReUnion), was known for its theatrical experiments. At the same time,
most contact improvisers felt they were part of a national movement.

From approximately 1976 to 1981, these localized developments
flourished and existed under the larger rubric of the informal national
organization: the *Contact Quarterly*, the touring network, the social network, and, beginning in 1976, the frequent occurrence of national workshops or retreats. During this period of time, participants experimented
with the techniques of the dance form and clarified ways of teaching
it. People also began to discuss extensively what contact improvisation
was about, investing it with a full range of meanings. Finally, granting
agencies and the press started to recognize contact improvisation, spurring local incorporations as not-for-profit organizations and encouraging
performance.

The growth infused the movement with a sense of purpose and
excitement. Issues of the *Quarterly* overflowed with letters of appreciation, reports of new classes and performances, reviews of contact improvisation reprinted from other publications, and poems, drawings, and
articles ranging from "Choreographing with Contact" to "The Politics
of Contact" to "The Teaching of Contact to Children with Learning
Disabilities." The magazine became a forum for the discussion of performing, teaching, and managing a company. Printing of the *Quarterly*

1. This general description does not always match actual performance practice. Steve
Paxton and Nancy Stark Smith, for example, presented improvised duets of simultaneous
talking and dancing, which they called dancetalk, during the mid-'70s.

increased from a first offset printing of three hundred fifty copies in the
spring of 1977 to fifteen hundred copies in 1980.

In 1977, Paxton, Nelson, Smith, Danny Lepkoff, Roger Neece, and
Elizabeth Zimmer formed Contact Collaborations, Inc., a nonprofit corporation, to assist the work of the magazine as well as to support the
rapidly growing video archives and to sponsor conferences. Through
that corporation, several National Endowment for the Arts grants were
obtained for the magazine, which Nancy Stark Smith and Lisa Nelson
(who became co-editor in 1978) have continued to edit.

The touring network expanded rapidly at this time. In the early
years, performers often lived out of their cars, working for little or no
money; by the middle and late '70s, some dancers were making a living
on tour with contact improvisation. Steve Paxton, Nancy Stark Smith,
and Mangrove (a San Francisco men's collective), among others, performed and taught for much of the year. ReUnion continued its annual
tour until 1978; in the meantime, Paxton toured with different combinations of people and performed with an ad hoc grouping called Free
Lance Dance (Paxton, Danny Lepkoff, Lisa Nelson, Nancy Stark Smith,
eventually Christina Svane). The emerging possibility of making money
through teaching and performing eventually affected contact improvisation, because it created a distinction between professional performers
and "just contact improvisers."

The social network maintained itself to a surprising degree despite
the expansion. Many people knew each other because of several sets
of circumstances. Touring brought people from different geographical
locations together. The *Contact Quarterly* enabled people to learn about
each other's work. The listing of "Contacts" in the back of the magazine
provided a social network which people used, even to the point of planning an itinerary for travel around it. "This network really worked," said
Ellen Elias. "You could call anybody listed in *CQ* and stay with them."
Contact improvisers felt that wherever they went, they would have someone with whom to live, talk, and dance.

An excerpt from a letter to *Contact Newsletter* in 1976 written by
Byron Brown of San Francisco and the company Mangrove conveys a
sense of the communal network surrounding contact improvisation in the
late '70s:

> Entering my contact year number three and living in the midst of
> what often seems to be the west coast center for contact improv.
> Number 224 here at the artists' warehouse called Project Artaud
> is a single large room with loft, kitchen, shower, 14 foot ceiling

and large open floor space. . . . John LeFan, his three year old son Krishna, and I share the space . . . often we share it with others, too. Seamus and Gail from Vancouver have both crashed here at different times ("contact contacts"); Mary from Minneapolis has been here for the past ten days during her SF visit; Storm, Shanti and others from Santa Cruz contacting have spent hours and nights while passing through. Bill Jones from Binghamton stopped in one afternoon to share some incredible dancing during his SF vacation; we look forward to many more guests. . . . This space has become a central meeting ground for business transaction. Mangrove eats and discusses here, is interviewed here, watches videotapes here and parties here. The Bay Area Contact Coalition formed initially for presenting Focus: 9/76 [a teaching workshop] has spent many hours . . . Last evening Roger Neece from the Boston improvisational company TA YU showed a small gathering a video of one of his company's performances; Curt showed a video of a Santa Cruz ReUnion performance. It was wonderful to feel the energy exchange across the continent. (*Contact Newsletter* 2[Fall 1976]:3)

The teaching workshops and conferences that brought dancers together from across the country and Canada constituted a final major force for maintaining social ties, as well as extended the techniques of the dance form. For instance, Nancy Stark Smith taught contact improvisation at Naropa Institute in Colorado every summer, teaching workshops in the San Francisco Bay Area were held every summer from 1976 to 1979, and the Vermont Movement Workshop, presenting contact improvisation and related techniques, occurred yearly.

Some events took on the nature of conferences: Nita Little, Nancy Stark Smith, members of Mangrove, and other Bay Area dancers organized the Contact Symposium in 1975 to dance and discuss ideas; Steve Paxton organized a retreat at Windham, Vermont, in 1977; Peter Ryan, a primary teacher in Vancouver, helped organize the Country Jam in 1979; Paxton gathered people for Current Exchange, a month-long retreat held in Vancouver, at which twenty-eight people danced, videotaped dancing, and talked about dancing, with no teachers or structures delineated explicitly. Significantly, throughout all these developments, the contact improvisers continued to think of themselves as largely unorganized. People exerted leadership and organized events in an implicit, casual way under the aegis of practicality and communication, carefully maintaining the ambiance of spontaneity and communal action.

40. Steve Paxton counterbalances with an unseen dancer. Photo © 1977 by Terry O'Reilly.

41. Terri Kruzan, *above*, and Tom Carlson of Contactworks, from Minneapolis. Photo © 1980 by Avis Mandel.

42. Andrew Harwood dances with Sean Hennessey in a contact improvisation workshop given by Harwood in Montreal. Photo © 1977 by André Denis.

43. David Woodberry, *above,* and Steve Paxton. Photo © 1977 by Stephen Petegorsky.

44. A performance of the San Francisco–based group, Mangrove, in Montreal, 1978. *From left to right,* Byron Brown, Rob Faust (*above*), Jim Tyler, and John LeFan. Courtesy of *Contact Quarterly.*

45. Free Lance Dance performing an improvisational structure called "Raft"
(1980). *From left to right,* Lisa Nelson, Nancy Stark Smith, and Christina Svane.
Photo © 1980 by Stephen Petegorsky.

46. The members of Free Lance Dance, 1980. *From left to right,* Christina Svane,
Steve Paxton, Nancy Stark Smith, Lisa Nelson, and Danny Lepkoff. Photo
© 1980 by Stephen Petegorsky.

47. Steve Paxton and Nancy Stark Smith performing together in 1984. Photo © 1984 by Bill Arnold.

48. Bill T. Jones, *above,* and Arnie Zane in their duet collaboration "Rotary Action" (1983). Photo © 1983 by Chris Harris.

However, the expansion of the form posed the problem of hierarchy in a number of ways. As a social form, anyone could dance with anyone else, no matter what their experience, and, in the early years, dancers who were almost beginners at contact improvisation performed with more experienced people. As the experienced people acquired more skill and as the form inevitably became less raw, the gap between an experienced person and a beginner widened. Maintaining a loose, egalitarian grouping grew more difficult. Ellen Elias remembered that "a lot of people got tired of dancing with beginners, even got tired of beatific looks on other people's faces." A discrepancy emerged between the values of openness and equality, the norms of a "folk" form in which anyone can participate, and the actual practices of some dancers trying to make a living as professional performers and others wanting simply to dance and have a good time.

"Generations" of contact improvisers also inevitably developed. For example, Mary Cerney, the Minneapolis dancer who had learned contact improvisation during a stay in California, taught classes back in Minneapolis in 1976. Some young dancers in her class, including Wendy Oliver, Patrick Scully, and Terri Kruzan, studied with her and became increasingly committed to the dance form. They had never seen the dancers whom they spoke of as the first generation—Nita Little, Steve Paxton, Danny Lepkoff—and they considered themselves "third-generation" contact improvisers.

The subsequent events in Minneapolis provide one example of what happened around the country in other cities. In 1976, Oliver and Scully, along with several other people, set up biweekly sessions to which anyone could come and practice contact improvisation outside of a class setting. Some of the dancers spent many hours each week practicing, and eventually they expressed a desire to perform. Within several months, they had consolidated as a group of five.

Some debate ensued about whether or not contact improvisation constituted a performance form. The Minneapolis dancers, who had all been trained previously in traditional dance forms, identified with Cerney's personal questioning of contact improvisation's focus on the internal state of the dancers rather than on the audience. Influenced by their previous teaching, they also wondered about the reliability of improvisation in performance and about the lack of composition in contact improvisation—the fact that "there was no beginning, middle, and end." These questions have been debated issues in the history of contact improvisation ever since its recognition as an actual form. Both participants and observers have talked about them, and the lack of resolution has been in part what keeps the dance form ambivalently straddled between social dance and art dance.[2]

Nevertheless, the Minneapolis dancers did start performing and, in 1977, applied for and received a ten thousand dollar grant from the Community Employment Training Act (C.E.T.A.) for a manager. They split the salary three ways among Oliver, JoAnne Tillemans, and Whitney Ray, who shared the administrative work and continued to rehearse and perform. Naming themselves Contactworks, the group existed as a company until 1981. During that time, a large contact improvisation community of over a hundred students and friends developed in Minneapolis. The contact jams continued on a regular basis, although eventually some participants in the jams complained that Contactworks dancers were being "elitist" because they no longer attended. "They didn't realize," recalled Scully, "that after teaching, rehearsing, performing, and doing arts administration work all week, we didn't often feel like getting out for two hours on a Sunday afternoon to dance."

Simultaneously, Oliver remembered, the members of Contactworks felt they formed part of "a wider national and international community." They obtained funding for major residencies by Nancy Stark Smith and members of Mangrove. Oliver also attended Focus and Crosscurrents, two of the national workshops, and the entire company performed at the Improvisation: Dance as Art-Sport conference in 1980.

The group never resolved the question of how to make contact improvisation more presentational and accessible to audiences. According to Scully, they remained dissatisfied with attempts to integrate contact improvisation with set choreography and compositional ideas, yet, by 1978, staying within the boundaries of contact improvisation made them feel constrained artistically. On the other hand, contact improvisation was their common bond, the basis for their collaboration, and it was their identity in public and the source of their community support and funding.

By 1981, people found that their individual goals were changing and that they were growing less oriented towards the group. Oliver, Scully, and Kruzan had all lived in collectives, which were disintegrat-

2. It is interesting to note, however, that these questions had not been raised by the dancers at the Weber Gallery, whose endeavor was supported by the ambiance of the New York avant-garde and by Steve Paxton's leadership.

ing (Oliver's lasted until 1984, but Scully and Kruzan's had disbanded in
1980). As a company, the members had worked collectively; in addition
to rehearsals and performances, they scheduled one hour a week for a
business meeting and one hour a week for group counseling. With five
days a week of rehearsal, the commitment was extensive. The strain of
administrating and dancing, coupled with changes in individuals' lives,
brought the group to an end. Wendy Oliver wrote me her analysis: "The
final dissolution of the group was largely due to collective burnout, a
need to explore personal interests, and a growing dissatisfaction with
being poor all the time."

The experience of Mangrove, the San Francisco–based performance
group, offers another example. Mangrove was founded by Byron Brown,
John LeFan, Jim Tyler, and Curt Siddall.[3] The first three dancers
had all been extensively involved with theater as well as dance. Brown
and LeFan had studied with Anna Halprin, and Brown had worked
with the Bread and Puppet Theatre. John LeFan had appeared in *Dionysus in '69* (and studied with the Performance Group director, Richard
Schechner) and had also trained with Ryszard Cieslak, an actor from
Grotowski's Polish Laboratory Theatre. Jim Tyler, who had been a member of the Erick Hawkins Dance Company, had studied with a number
of improvisational acting teachers in the United States and Europe.

With so much performance experience, the members of Mangrove
became active very quickly. As cosponsors of the Focus Workshops (teaching sessions held in the summers of 1976 and 1977), and as sole sponsors
of the Mangrove teaching sessions held in the summers of 1978 and 1979,
they were very influential teachers. Mangrove also probably constituted
the most active, single performing contact improvisation group in existence, presenting some two hundred fifty performances over a five-year
period in the United States, Canada, and Europe.

Their extensive activity as a company eventually led to some conflict between Mangrove and other contact improvisers in the Bay Area,
similar to rifts between Contactworks and the rest of the contact improvisation community in Minneapolis. In the early years of contact improvisation in the Bay Area, loose associations among participants had been
formed in order to make performances possible; now, Mangrove was a
set and separate group. When Mangrove presented its own teaching sessions in 1978 rather than joining with others, teachers and performers

3. By 1978, Siddall had left to become a carpenter and Charles Campbell, Rob Faust,
Ernie Adams, and Bob Rease had joined the collective.

unaffiliated with a company were resentful. Mangrove finally disbanded in 1980, although individuals continued to develop their own work and to perform.

In contact improvisation communities across the country, whatever negative feelings may have existed in the movement during the late '70s were generally aired through personal channels, although some heated discussions and disagreements appeared in the magazine. For example, Mark Pritchard, a San Francisco dancer, wrote an article for *Contact Quarterly* criticizing what he saw as the rigid association of contact improvisation by its proponents with certain other practices like "holistic health" or "therapy" and a tendency towards self-justification on the basis of being "natural." Pritchard warned that the contact community was becoming passive and self-righteous, viewing going with the "'flow' of natural events" as "the best way to do anything . . . rather than attempting to shape those events on one's own" (*Contact Quarterly* 6[Fall 1980]:5). Byron Brown wrote a respectful reply, addressing Pritchard's questions indirectly by discussing the range of possibilities for contact improvisation as a performance form in evidence at the 1980 "art-sport" conference (*Contact Quarterly* 6[Fall 1980]:6–9).

For the most part, however, the public decorum and open-mindedness encouraged by the values and norms of contact improvisation tempered the expression of conflict. On the whole, the *Contact Quarterly* served primarily as a unifying mechanism for a diverse, occasionally diverging, movement.

Improvisation: Dance as Art-Sport Conference

In June 1980, contact improvisation aficionado and dance writer Elizabeth Zimmer, who was also director of the American Dance Guild, helped arrange a national conference, Improvisation: Dance as Art-Sport, which was originally set up as a contact improvisation conference. The Dance Guild Board of Directors expanded the topic of the conference to dance improvisation in general, but Steve Paxton remained the keynote speaker. This conference included classes, panel discussions, and performances, and more than three hundred improvisers attended, over a third of them contact improvisers, from the United States, Canada, and Europe. In retrospect, the conference represents a kind of peak in the contact improvisation movement as an active national organization.

Over the five-day period, some sixty people offered nearly seventy class sessions relating to improvisation. Six classes dealt directly with con-

tact improvisation; other classes fell into the categories of structuring
and generating improvisation, new games and sport and their relationship to dance improvisation, methods of teaching and practicing dance
therapy, and movement awareness techniques. Three concerts were presented in which fifteen different companies or groups appeared. There
were also panel discussions, informal meetings, a banquet, and a closing
ceremony directed by Anna Halprin, recipient of a Dance Guild award
at the conference.

Of the improvisational companies or ad hoc groups which performed, nine were from the contact improvisation movement. The
performances demonstrated the range of interpretations of contact improvisation: Catpoto, a women's group from Montreal, presented a pre-
choreographed dance which they had developed through contact improvisation; Men Working and Mirage, two collectives from Michigan, did
"pure" contact performances; Free Lance Dance mixed contact improvisation with other kinds of improvised dancing; and Byron Brown and
Nancy Stark Smith, who had seldom danced together before, performed
a contact improvisation duet.

Most contact improvisers were extremely enthusiastic about the conference, seeing it as a confirmation of their movement, although a few
were dismayed at performances which they did not consider sufficiently
serious.[4] The extensive performing impressed the majority of people,
even if they did not like everything they saw. The conference also presented a stimulus for new experimentation because of the range of dancing it displayed and because of the number of kinds of people, contact
improvisers and other kinds of improvisers as well, which it included.

Steve Paxton's keynote address also confirmed a sense of leadership
and history for contact improvisation. Paxton's talk comprised a series of
musings on the nature of improvisation (Paxton 1980). He spoke about
performance as behavior, a chance "to observe oneself" reacting spontaneously, as opposed to performance as preplanned presentation. He con-
templated the "wall" of one's own movement habits encountered when
supposedly "dancing freely," and he discussed the concept of "ki" (in
Eastern philosophy, the energy source from the earth manifested in the
body) in doing improvisation. Paxton, apparently reluctant to assume the
role of "guru" yet unable to avoid the respect and even awe so many at

4. Participants voiced two kinds of complaints: the dancers either "clowned too much,"
going after laughs and losing the integrity of the contact interaction, or the dancers were
simply not very skilled. One very experienced dancer said, "Some of the contact improvisation felt shallow and it hurt to see that. . . . I was putting my life behind it."

the conference felt towards him, tried to minimize his authority by quali-
fying his statements, pausing a lot, and moving away from the podium
partway through his address to sit at the edge of the stage. As usual with
Paxton's attempts to back out of the limelight, people admired him all
the more for it.

The momentum resulting from the conference, however, proved in-
sufficient to cohere the increasing divergence of the movement or to alter
the changes occurring in people's lives. Ellen Elias, convinced at the conference that a book should be written about contact improvisation, tried
to organize a collective effort, with chapters written by different people
or groups of people. Although individuals received her proposal with
enthusiasm, only one person actually wrote anything for her.

The *Quarterly* continued to publish, but it printed fewer articles directly about contact improvisation. The magazine provided less evidence
of an active movement and developed into more of a forum for discussions relating to the concepts of contact improvisation—articles about
teaching, kinesiology, choreography, and body therapy. Increasingly, the
two editors (Smith and Nelson) took virtually all responsibility for publishing the journal, because they were no longer able to count on an active
national community of involved dancers to write for it.

The contact improvisation movement seemed to be in a state of tran-
sition. Among the contact improvisation groups which had been listed in
the 1978 "Performance" issue of the *Contact Quarterly* or had appeared at
the Art-Sport conference, none remained in existence by 1982.

Contact at 10th and 2nd

Indications of the directions in which contact improvisation might have
been moving were apparent at the national conference on contact improvisation held in June 1983. Steve Paxton organized Contact at 10th and
2nd in New York City at St. Mark's Church by sending letters inviting
people to come and show what they were doing. The conference consisted largely of nine evening performances, open to the public. One
panel discussion occurred, and one large contact jam. The continuities
and changes from 1972 to 1983 became clear during these events.

In the panel discussion at the St. Mark's conference, many of the
ideas expressed were familiar from the early days of the contact improvisation movement. People discussed the physical reality of exchanging
weight, the value of the social network, and the egalitarian nature of the

form. However, they voiced less concern in 1983 about "allowing" the dance to happen and instead raised questions about what had been "left out" of contact improvisation ("attention to emotions, eroticism, will or intention") that might now be included.

The panel discussion was perhaps more fascinating in its structure than in its content. Following the ambiguous, informal, implicit mode of organization typical of contact improvisation, no one introduced the panelists and no one seemed to know when to begin. Finally, Steve Paxton spoke, presenting the format upon which a planning group had collectively decided: the discussion would start with everyone but eventually pairs of panelists would go off with members of the audience for smaller discussion groups. A row of tape recorders lined the front of the panelists' table so that the small-group meetings could be documented as well as the initial large-group one, but the entire plan to split into smaller groups never materialized. Throughout the discussion, Paxton sometimes played a very active, even combative, role, responding and questioning; at several points, however, he unexpectedly and without explanation left the room, apparently to do something with the jam which was occurring in the adjoining space.

After the discussion, which was quite scattered and inconclusive, two different people involved in the planning told me that the meeting to organize the discussion had been very exciting and that, somehow, the actual event never achieved the same dynamic. The planning meeting succeeded as an unstructured improvisation, but the larger event seemed to present too many underlying hierarchies and conflicting intentions to work well without a more elaborate structure or a director.

In the performances, the basic characteristics of the dancing remained evident. Contact improvisation still largely concerned the give and take of weight between two or more dancers using momentum and gravity. "Pure" contact duets and group dances characterized some of the performances; a mixture of contact improvisation with other kinds of improvisation, with dramatic ideas, or with conceptual frameworks characterized others.

Yet the execution of the dancing, the particular styles in which the basic structure was realized, had changed. Contact improvisation by now constituted an extremely technically developed dance form requiring great skill to perform. The dancers spun out long phrases of movement which were far more fluid, soft, and controlled than the earlier dancing. They had learned how to do extraordinary lifts and falls in a finely

articulated, often sustained way, as opposed to the rough, sudden movement in the mid-'70s. Although the dancing was playful and sometimes
surprising, it was seldom "dangerous" or totally unpredictable; no matter what the risks, the dancers were experienced enough to transform
them into controlled movements. These changes had to do with developments in movement technique, an increase in presentational qualities in
the performing, changes in relationships among the dancers, and shifts
in the meanings or significances of certain kinds of movement events.
What was once culturally shocking and electrifying was now entertaining
and touching.

The audience response reaffirmed these changes. Hundreds of
people attended the performances and virtually always received them
warmly. While the audience was more voluble than that at most modern
dance concerts, the general tenor was of fond appreciation, very different
from the atmosphere of charged, shared energy described as charac-
terizing early contact improvisation concerts. Contact improvisation was
no longer new, the meanings of movement had changed, and the social
attitude of audiences had shifted from communal engagement with the
dancers to a more removed contemplation of the performance.

On the last evening of the conference, seven dancers performed in
an open session: David Appel, Robin Feld, Steve Paxton, Alan Ptashek,
Nancy Stark Smith, Kirstie Simson, and Peter Ryan. They were working
all together as a group for the first time, although some people knew
each other extremely well and had danced together often. A videotape
of the performance made by Michael Schwartz offers a kind of summary
statement of contact improvisation in 1983 and characterizes the general
movement style through the '80s.

The recurring transitional theme in "Contact at 10th and 2nd" is
a run or a walk around the edge of the space, often with one or more
people linked arm in arm or, towards the end of the performance, carrying each other. Duets and trios break off, sometimes dancing simultaneously and even interchanging personnel, more often settling into
movement sequences of from three to ten minutes.

The overriding qualities in this event are virtuoso performances
combined with an attitude of congenial, relaxed playfulness and a low-
key sense of performance. The dancers display extraordinary skills,
making very dangerous and difficult interactions look easy. These performers seem able both physically and choreographically to absorb sudden changes. Perhaps two obviously jarring or dangerous falls occur in

the entire performance in which someone might have gotten injured. At one point, Paxton takes a hard fall onto his hands. At another, Ryan pulls Smith in a whiplash backward arc over his thigh, and she flashes him a quick but potent warning look as they continue dancing. Otherwise, the movement appears "in control" even at its wildest moments, because these dancers apparently can handle anything. Choreographically, the dancers investigate interesting possibilities, reacting with contrasting dynamics to another's sudden change, or picking up duet movement and performing it alone.

The give-and-take of weight no longer constitutes the sole subject matter of the dancing. This dance concerns *how* weight is given, how much is given, and with what attitude. In a sense, the dance encompasses the entire range of touch, from the lightest contact to full body weight, and even extending to the "contact" of eye focus across the space. Furthermore, the range of movement outside of actual body contact is extensive, so that the element of improvisation emerges as strongly as does the body contact.

Minute and complete body-part articulation, in largely successive movement, characterizes the use of the body. The dancers employ every conceivable part of the body as means of support on the floor and on each other. They also seem able to combine an inward orientation and awareness with consciously shaping and designing the body in space. Although dancers move through a great range of body shapes and pathways in space, this contact improvisation appears more vertical than earlier versions. The dancers have a greater ability to support one another when standing upright; they have the skills to balance a person on their shoulders or to spiral someone down an upright body.

As the performers' orientation to space outside of the body increases, so does their attention to time, which seems much more consciously drawn out or hurried up than in even the Northampton performance. Because of the predominance of attention to time, less evidence of the simple use of weight and movement flow (what Laban called the dream state) appears than in earlier dancing. Although the dancing looks relaxed, it is also highly athletic and exuberant, with sections of agitated jostling, shaking, and flinging movement. In fact, this agitation seems to have been added to the repertoire of solo dancing in contact improvisation; soloists often move suddenly, articulating different body parts and sending them off in different directions, lurching and following through after their own momentum. The initiation of movement from a range of different body parts which typifies the duet interaction has become transferred into the solo work, producing surprising movement sequences at once twitching and fluid, disjointed and delicate.

Finally, this event definitely has the character of a performance in the sense that the dancers seem quite aware of the audience. They make a number of dance jokes for the audience's benefit, as well as for each other. Paxton slides Ryan back and forth on the floor, holding him by the feet, as if he were a vacuum cleaner, and when they later inadvertently wind up in this same position, Ryan signals a "time-out" with his hands. In a subsequent duet between Ryan and Smith, they make two more references to the vacuum cleaner. Feld and Appel parody a ballet *pas de deux* at one point. Shortly after that, Paxton and Feld dance together, jiggling and jostling like two mad characters. Paxton suddenly looks at her dramatically, absurdly, and the two of them part, staring intently at each other as the audience howls with laughter at the surrealism of this pseudodramatic event in the middle of a contact improvisation. She falls forward, flat onto the ground. He lifts her stiffly held body perpendicular to his and spins rapidly, shifting easily and suddenly back into context. He sets her on her feet, and they walk off arm in arm.

The Continuing Practice of Contact Improvisation

Despite the disintegration of many contact improvisation companies and the dissolution of communal life-styles in the late '70s and early '80s, people did not stop doing contact improvisation. New centers and companies formed; for example, Eugene, Oregon, and Seattle, Washington, were active locations for contact improvisation throughout the '80s. Activities in Vancouver and Montreal flourished in a Canadian dance world without a strongly established modern dance tradition. In New York City, contact improvisation classes have fluctuated in size but have always rebuilt after periods of small attendance. The jams have continued in many cities, as have regional and national dance sessions.

At the same time, aspects of the technique of contact improvisation have permeated modern dance. Contact improvisation has formed the basis for many improvisational or partly improvised performances (for example, in the work of Channel Z, David Woodberry, David Appel, Fred Holland, Ishmael Houston-Jones, Jennifer Monson, Yvonne Meier, Daniel Lepkoff, Steve Krieckhaus, Alan Ptashek, and Laurie Booth). More pervasively, choreographers have adapted the movement style and

49. *From left to right,* Louise Parent, Paula Doshe, and Dena Davida in "Pièce de Résistance" (1986). Photo © 1986 by Donna Marie Marchand. Courtesy of Dena Davida.

50. A performance by teachers at the annual A Cappella Workshop in
Northampton, 1987. *From left to right*, Carol Swann, Andrew Harwood, and
Susan Schell. Photo © 1987 by Bill Arnold.

51. Alito Alessi and Karen Nelson in "Hoop Dance" (1988). Photo © 1988 by Cliff Coles.

52. Performers in Nina Martin's "Modern Daze" (1988). *From left to right,* Theresa Reeves, Margery Segal, David Maier, and Terry O'Reilly. Photo © 1988 by Dona Ann McAdams.

53. Channel Z in 1986. *From left to right,* Danny Lepkoff, Randy Warshaw, Paul Langland, Nina Martin (*above*), and Diane Madden. Photo © 1986 by Dona Ann McAdams.

partnering skills into set choreography (for example, in the work of Bill T. Jones, Robin Feld, Karen Nelson and Alito Alessi, Nina Martin, the Wallflower Order, Stephanie Skura, Johanna Boyce, Edward Locke, Dena Davida, Mark Thomkins, Terry Creach and Stephen Koester, Kinematic, Randy Warshaw, and Stephen Petronio). The general movement style of dancers in many companies evidences contact improvisation training. This is the case for many of the choreographers just mentioned, as well as for others like Trisha Brown and Twyla Tharp, who used a number of dancers in the early '80s who had studied contact improvisation. Choreographers have also taught contact improvisation to actors and ballet dancers: in Vancouver, Peter Ryan has used it as a catalyst for performing scenes from Shakespeare, and Freddy Long, Jim Tyler, and John LeFan created a piece (1985) for the San Francisco Ballet Company. Contact improvisation has helped shape a general transformation in theater dance movement style which greatly affected the look of performance in the late '70s and through the '80s.

A description written in a letter by Peter Ryan in 1988 of recent choreography which he and Peter Bingham had been directing in Vancouver, suggests some of the ways in which choreographers have adapted and developed contact improvisation:

> Peter Bingham has actually spent parts of this year in going back to the basic form of Contact, stripping it of the inevitable accretions that years of work can apply. He has been working with a group of dancers, most of whom were trained by Peter and me, and they are currently performing Contact in a manner close to the way it was presented in the seventies. One of his primary reasons for doing this was, he said, to rediscover the place, or state, where the dance itself would carry the dancers through, rather than the imposed notion of "performing" Contact.
>
> This group of performers has also been presenting more theatrically-staged work that is still largely Contact-based, in that the primary vocabulary and the sensibility derives from the techniques and attitudes instilled by the disciplined practice of Contact. . . .
>
> Peter has used Contact in choreographed work, finding it to be a rich source of movement material for his more structured ideas. In all this, group awareness, timing, and spacing between people have derived from the inherent compositional

flow provided by Contact when it is practiced without conscious manipulation or for its more splashy effects.

. . . I've also been working on ensemble improvisation with a group of three actors and three dancers, using Contact as a metaphor for community and the social fabric. The piece, "Ceremony of Innocence," is set in Germany in the 1930's at a time when social mores and traditions are crumbling under pressures of the political movements of both Nazism and Communism. In a tightly structured context, Contact becomes a means whereby the inner states of people can be experienced externally. (Personal communication)

Contact improvisation has also formed a basis for dance organizations of a social nature, not only jams, but also regular occasions of "free" dancing held in many cities. On the East Coast, for example, two of these dance organizations have become significant features in the dance community. One is Open Movement, an evening of dancing which occurs every Tuesday night, year round, at Performance Space 122 in New York City. Actors associated with the Byrd Hoffman School started the session in 1974, and in 1979 Charles Dennis situated the event at P.S. 122. Increasingly, the people attending it have studied contact improvisation, and that dance form has come to constitute a basis for much of the activity.

A second dance organization on the East Coast actually has comprised a larger network of a number of dance collectives in different cities. The network, called Dance New England, coalesced in 1980 when people from New Haven and Boston decided to join their collectives for a weekend of dance classes. The network grew by 1985 to include over five hundred people from New York, Hartford, Providence, and smaller towns in the New England area. Beginning in 1981, it has collectively sponsored four weekends of classes a year in different locations and a ten-day summer camp. The group has consisted largely of nonperforming dancers for whom contact improvisation has become both a major component of their dance experience and a strong metaphor for the way in which they try to run their communities.

Many contact improvisers have commented on the change in ambiance in the culture at large which they feel has affected contact improvisation. Nina Martin, who danced in ad hoc contact groups in New York City in the late '70s (the "hippie days," as she put it), stopped doing contact improvisation for a while because of an injury and because she was interested in doing more than "pure" contact improvisation in performance. "When I pulled back from [performing] the form," Martin said, "I thought other people would fill in, but they didn't." Martin was teaching classes at the time and offered to direct a group of students in collective work. What might have been a golden opportunity for students in the early '70s was not seized in 1980; Martin felt the students lacked the desire to work through something together on a sustained basis and perform it. "They had started getting the drift for how to have a professional career in dance," Martin suggested, and collective endeavors consequently were less appealing to them than individual ones.

Martin herself eventually returned to collective work which had a basis in contact improvisation. In 1983, she started dancing with a group in New York known as Channel Z. It included Danny Lepkoff (one of the original Weber dancers), Paul Langland (a contact improviser in 1973 at Bennington), and Diane Madden and Randy Warshaw (contact improvisers from Hampshire College, 1978–80); the original group also included Robin Feld and Stephen Petronio. Channel Z provides one example of an improvisational group working in the '80s which did not say it was doing contact improvisation but derived much of its style and conception from contact improvisation. In 1985, Martin said that Channel Z did not advertise that they did improvisation at all because "as a career, it won't work. Critics don't come, or come and don't write about it. They look at it [improvisation] as a cultural, educational experience, not something worthy of being written about."

The demonstrations of the early years no longer seemed feasible in the '80s. By 1984, contact improvisation had largely become divided into its parts; what was once a union of an art form and a social form had become either a movement technique for performance or a social, recreational activity. The division was not a complete one, but it clearly existed.

Nancy Stark Smith, the most active touring teacher and performer of contact improvisation, talked in 1984 about the trends she observed:

> It's true that the times are different. What happens, it seems to
> me, are two diametrically opposed things. One is that the individu-
> als become more prominent, so that you're not just going to go to
> a contact improvisation performance, but you might go to see one
> person and not another. . . . At the same time, people talk about

community more. When there *was* a community, nobody talked about it at all. It's like when you live in a family, you don't have to talk to your brother about your family all the time. But as the family starts breaking up, you get nostalgic and you say, "Oh, we were such a great family, everyone was so close," which, of course, is usually not quite true either.

Smith's comments point to the fascinating dialectic between art forms and social life. The cultural ambiance in 1972 allowed for the development of a dance form like contact improvisation and made it possible for Paxton, Smith, and the early contact improvisers to accomplish what they did artistically and socially. The dance form was imbued with cultural and social meaning. It became a cultural text that generated readings by its participants and its audiences, and it offered a cultural scenario that provided models for action. Years later, the dance form allowed people to invoke a social ambiance from the past, even though both artistic and social circumstances had changed. As John LeFan commented in 1988, "Contact improvisation is still to me representative of a way of life that I would like to emulate."

5
Movement and Meaning in Contact Improvisation

The descriptions of performances of contact improvisation in the two previous chapters evidence a gradual transformation of an initially raw form into a more polished, articulate style. Some of the changes appear to have derived from the process of working over a long period of time on particular skills: people acquired greater control, more subtlety, and refinement. Practical concerns also spurred change; most significantly the need to exchange weight without getting hurt or hurting one's partner stimulated technical developments, particularly when it became impossible to work with a mat on a regular basis. Thus, dancers focused on how to control and soften the actions of falling, rolling, catching, and supporting.

Other technical changes seem to indicate deliberate choices to employ particular movement qualities or to strive for a certain kind of encounter. For example, dancers early on consciously attempted to extend the length of the duet, spurring discovery of how to keep the movement flow going. By 1978, the notion of ongoing flow had assumed major importance; also, choreographic ideas were entering into the practice of the form. By 1982, dancers seemed less concerned with doing *only* contact improvisation in a performance, and though the give and take of weight was still at the heart of the performance, how the weight exchange occurred seemed equally important.

Summary of the Movement Style

Throughout this history of change, the basic style of the dancing which has identified it immediately as contact improvisation has remained. In order to discuss the implications of that style and to understand changes in its interpretation and practice through time, an image or vision of the style must be clear.

Movement analyst Billie Frances Lepczyk has suggested that every movement style has a particular "coloring" of the "dynamic image" it presents, a constellation of qualities which characterize it and render its style immediately recognizable. By describing the "core movement values" which constitute "the baseline of the movement style," Lepczyk suggests, one can arrive at a better articulation of the dynamic image of a movement form (Lepczyk 1981:7).[1] The following summary enumerates the core movement values of contact improvisation, as well as its organization and performance frame.[2]

Generating movement through the changing points of contact between bodies: Predominance of two bodies moving while touching, finding a mutual spatial pathway for movement through the interaction of body weight. Movement is guided by the dancers' sense of how to maintain body contact and continue the exchange of support. (See illustration 54.)

Sensing through the skin: Use of all surfaces of the body to support one's own weight and the weight of another person; almost constant maintenance of touch between partners. (See illustrations 55 and 56.)

Rolling through the body; focus on segmenting the body and moving in several directions simultaneously: Successive or sequential (one after the other) use of body parts, coupled with sending the body in several different

---

1. The concept of core qualities is central to Irmgard Bartenieff's work (1980).

2. My movement analysis was made over a period of several years, viewing videotapes and performances and using concepts from the work of Rudolf Laban (1971, 1974) and Irmgard Bartenieff (1980). The analysis was facilitated by using "coding sheets," lists of qualities about which to make observations and record impressions systematically. Discussions with Tara McClellan, CMA (certified movement analyst), were extremely helpful in making my analysis, as was access to her unpublished manuscript on contact improvisation (1980). Diane Woodruff, CMA, also assisted me in designing coding sheets and in analyzing portions of the videotapes, and Robert Ellis Dunn, CMA, has been an invaluable resource in understanding Laban Movement Analysis.

54. *Generating movement through the changing points of contact between bodies*:
This photo of Diane Madden and Randy Warshaw may at first appear to be a
ballroom dance, but close examination reveals that Warshaw is falling lightly
against Madden's leg and a third dancer's back (Eleanor Huston). The other
points at which the bodies are in contact (two hands, arm, and waist) are being
used to sense the mutual support and release of weight. Many possible actions
could follow this one, but the choices will be guided by maintaining body
contact and continuing the exchange of support. Photo © 1979 by Stephen
Petegorsky.

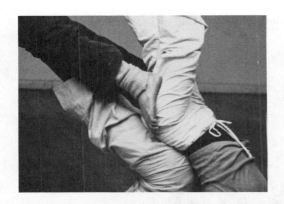

55 and 56. *Sensing through the skin*: Illustration 55 shows a range of supporting surfaces used by three dancers, Andrew Harwood, Helen Clarke, and Peter Bingham of Fulcrum; illustration 56 shows Steve Paxton using a well-chosen point on Nancy Stark Smith's leg and a balancing hand on her shoulder to support his weight. In both of these examples, the dancers know through their sense of touch where and when weight can be safely given and support can be safely offered. Illustration 55 © 1978 by Chris Randle. Illustration 56 © 1977 by Ted Pushinsky.

57. *Rolling through the body*: Steve Paxton and Nancy Stark Smith's twisting actions in which shoulders and head appear to move first while the rest of the body remains temporarily behind are typical of contact improvisation. Photo © 1977 by Ted Pushinsky.

directions at once. The flow of continuous transitions through neighboring segments allows for increased improvisational options with a partner and for softer landings from falls and rolls. The segmenting of the body and the multiple focus of direction gives a jointed appearance to the movement.[3] (See illustration 57.)

3. Traditional modern dance forms like Humphrey or Graham technique also roll through the body successively, but they tend to focus in a single direction or on simple opposition, giving them an appearance of "organic" smoothness and follow-through. Differences in the effects of successiveness also derive from the way energy is applied: the greater control exerted over the movement in traditional techniques contrasts with the frequent use of freely flowing momentum in contact improvisation.

58. *Experiencing movement from the inside*: The supporting partner (Nancy Stark Smith) focuses inwardly as she concentrates on moving forward while the weight of her partner (Steve Paxton) balances on her shoulder. Paxton combines his internal attention with arching his legs and head into space. Photo © 1978 by Bill Arnold.

Experiencing movement from the inside: Orientation or focus inward, sensing the internal space of the body; secondary attention (depending on the performer) to shaping the body in space. Contact improvisers have this internal focus a good deal of the time in order to perceive subtle weight changes and not endanger themselves or others. Skilled contact improvisers, to whom a sensing of weight becomes almost second nature, tend more often to intentionally project their bodies into the surrounding space than beginners do. At the same time, even people doing solos in a contact performance often retain an internal focus and absorption in the sensation of moving. (See illustration 58.)

59. *Using 360-degree space*: The curved trajectories of the falling bodies are evident (Nancy Stark Smith and Alan Ptashek). Photo © 1979 by Erich Franz.

Using 360-degree space: Three-dimensional pathways in space, making
   spiraling, curved, or circular lines with the body.[4] These pathways
   are closely connected to the physical properties of lifting weight and
   falling with minimal exertion. Lifting in an arc requires less muscle strength and falling in an arc decreases the downward impact.
   (See illustration 59.)

   4. Laban conceived of movement in the physical world as organizing itself spatially
along lines of crystalline structures. Tara McClellan (1980) has suggested that contact improvisation is one of the only dance forms to organize itself almost entirely within the
icosahedron, a crystalline form with twenty-four points (break dancing is another). Many
dance forms relate far more to the vertical axis running up and down through the body,
focusing on the independent upright figure; their spatial pathways tend to be octahedral or
planal and stress the dimensional axes (e.g., ballet or Cunningham) or cubelike and stress
the diagonal axes (e.g., Graham).

60. *Going with the momentum, emphasizing weight and flow*: Sylvie St. Laurent easily supports Dena Davida because of the mutual momentum of St. Laurent's initial push and/or Davida's initial jump. Photo © 1978 by André Denis.

Going with the momentum, emphasizing weight and flow: Preponderance of free or ongoing movement flow coupled with alternation of active use of weight and passive weight. Contact improvisers often emphasize continuity of movement without knowing exactly where the movement will take them. They may actively push, pull, or lift to

61. *Tacit inclusion of the audience; conscious informality of presentation, modeled on a practice or jam*: Steve Paxton and Nancy Stark Smith in a studio performance space typical of the presentation of contact improvisation, in which the dancers and audience are very close to each other. The dancers wear practice clothes, and the space is bare of stage lights or set; the video documenter sits at the edge. Many of the other illustrations of contact improvisation in this book indicate conscious informality. Photo © 1975 by Edmund Shea.

follow the thrust of energy, or passively allow momentum to carry them. (See illustration 60.)

Tacit inclusion of the audience; conscious informality of presentation, modeled on a practice or jam: Proximity to the audience, seating usually in the round with no formal stage space. Particularly in the early years of contact improvisation, dancing would be going on when the audience entered, so that the beginning of the performance was indefinite. This performance setup simulates the contact jam, as does the lack of production values (light, props, sets, programs) and the "costumes," which are practice clothes. (See illustration 61.)

The dancer is just a person: Adoption of a behavioral, or "natural," stance: dancers generally avoid movements clearly identified with traditional dance techniques and do not distinguish between "everyday movement" and "dancing"; they adjust clothing, scratch, laugh, or

62. *The dancer is just a person*: Most of the photographs of contact improvisation in this book indicate an absence of movements identified with traditional modern dance or ballet techniques. The deliberate gaze of the kneeling dancer (Danny Lepkoff) is an example of a "natural" gesture occurring within the dance. The other dancer pictured is Steve Paxton. Photo © 1977 by Stephen Petegorsky.

    cough whenever necessary (and sometimes even when not necessary in order to signal informality); they generally do not look at the audience. (See illustration 62.)

Letting the dance happen: Choreographic organization structured by sequence of duets, sometimes trios or larger groups, and almost continuous physical interaction of performers. Choreographic elements such as organization of space, establishment of movement themes, or the use of dramatic gesture are seldom pursued intentionally,

63. *Letting the dance happen*: The choreographic shaping which can arise from contact improvisation is particularly difficult to illustrate with a photograph, but illustration 63 can be seen to represent a kind of interaction which forms groupings and events. Dancers pictured, *from left to right,* are Julyen Hamilton, Nancy Stark Smith, Andrew Harwood, and Kirstie Simson. Photo © 1985 by Bill Arnold.

but choreographic shaping does arise from the dynamic of changing personnel and the emergence of particular moods and qualities in the improvisation. (See illustration 63.)

Everyone should be equally important: Lack of external signs of differentiation between dancers such as order of appearance, length of dancing time, costuming. The movement qualities of contact improvisation often reinforce this message. (See illustration 64.)

64. *Everyone should be equally important*: Dancers are not distinguished by external signs of relative importance or unimportance, as seen in this photograph of four people. Photo © 1986 by Bill Arnold.

Ballet and Contact Improvisation

A comparison between the movement styles of contact improvisation and ballet, a dance form more familiar to many readers, may help to evoke further the qualities of contact improvisation. The comparison also raises issues of meaning, because the two dance forms, which seem antithetical on the surface, share a basic similarity: both include a duet structure as a central component. Examining the way each form shapes the duet reveals constraints surrounding gender roles in American culture and the ways in which those roles are embodied in movement.[5]

A man and a woman always dance the ballet duet, the *pas de deux*,

5. As movement and bodies are always culturally shaped, so too are movement differences which become classified as masculine and feminine. Research on these differences has been concentrated in the field of nonverbal communication, which has analyzed "body language" in social situations. For example, Raymond Birdwhistell (1970), as part of his kinesic analysis of social coding, compared gender distinctions in seven different societies. He concluded not only that a range of masculine and feminine behaviors exist cross-culturally but also that "natives" can identify "male" movement and "female" movement and can easily detect "different degrees of accentuation or diminution of such movement depending upon the situation" (43).

65. Fernando Bujones, of the American Ballet Theatre, lifts Yoko Morishita as she smiles out to the audience. Both dancers control the shape of their bodies so that a momentary pose can be presented to the spectator. Photo © 1983 by Johan Elbers.

66. This photograph shows the reverse of the gender roles in illustration 65, with Karen Nelson lifting Alito Alessi. The movement indicated by the two photos also contrasts; whereas the ballet duet is more controlled and shape oriented, the contact improvisation duet is more ongoing and oriented towards dynamic flow. Photo © 1988 by Cliff Coles.

establishing heterosexuality as the norm, particularly because the encounter most often refers to romantic love. Partnering in ballet means
that the man guides, supports, carries, and manipulates the woman.[6]
Thus a sexual division of labor in movement characterizes the *pas de deux:*
usually, the man is solid, stable, and strong, while the woman is delicately
balanced on one leg, her limbs extended in the air. This gendered codification of movement maintains itself outside of the *pas de deux*. The male
soloist tends to exhibit strength in large jumps and air turns, whereas the
female soloist tends to exhibit flexibility and quickness in leg extensions
and footwork. Even the "abstract" ballets of George Balanchine, which
contain no narrative, follow these same movement conventions.

The contact improvisation duet, on the other hand, may take place
between a man and a woman, two women, or two men, and it does not
attempt to represent romantic love or any other narrative content. The
dance form has no gendered codification of movement vocabulary; the
vocabulary that exists (such as rolling, falling, counterbalancing) is available for both men and women.

Ballet requires exaggerated sexual dimorphism because the man
must be able to lift the woman with ease. For women, lightness and
flexibility in a slender, long-limbed, strong but fragile-looking body are
desirable. For men, strength and agility in a lean but muscular body are
valued. As a rule, the male body must be larger and taller than the female
body.

In a contact improvisation duet, each member, male or female, must
be ready to give or take weight, to support, to resist, or to yield, as called
for by the interaction. Any kind of male or female body is acceptable,
because the form depends on sensing momentum and changing from
active to passive weight at the right moments; a large person who knows
how to move his or her weight may seem much lighter than a small person who does not. That a person is a man or woman, smaller or larger,
is not a central concern of the dancers.

In addition, a shared movement style for men and women characterizes each dance form. In the ballet, movement is generally presentational

6. Ann Daly (1987a) provides a detailed analysis of the partnering in the third opening theme of Balanchine's "Four Temperaments," asking if the structure of ballet is in-
herently sexist (also see Daly 1987–88). Studies of American gender-role patterning have
pointed to the frequent convergence of female-subordinate and male-dominant movement
codes in situations in which negotiations of social power are involved (Birdwhistell 1970;
Scheflen 1972; Henley 1977). Erving Goffman (1976) has argued that the "choreography"
of gender stereotypes in advertising shapes materials drawn from the society at large (albeit
in a distorted fashion) and, in turn, influences people's "choreography" of their lives.

and outwardly focused; it emphasizes the periphery of the body (the arms, legs, and head), the spatial design of the body (its shape), and the control of the vertical balance. In contact improvisation, movement is generally focused internally, rather than towards an audience; it emphasizes the center of the body (the torso), the weight and momentum or energy flow of the body, and the ability to lose one's balance, to fall off the vertical.

Costumes often reinforce distinctions between men and women in ballet, but they obscure these distinctions in contact improvisation. Ballet costumes highlight signs of sexual identity; they display bare arms and decolletage of the women, legs and pelvis of men and women. Ballet costumes also indicate hierarchy among the male and female dancers, because the soloist usually wears a costume or color different from the *corps de ballet*. The contact improvisers' anticostumes of "work" clothes,

67. These male dancers from Les Ballets Trockadero de Monte Carlo exaggerate the codes of femininity as they perform "Les Sylphides." The photograph quickly makes a theoretical point that sexual identity (being male or female), sexuality, and gender roles can be considered separately (Caplan 1987:20). Photo © 1983 by Johan Elbers.

68. London's Royal Ballet dances "Sleeping Beauty," a ballet first choreographed in 1889. It tells the famous story of romantic love in which only a
prince can awaken the princess Aurora from the evil spell cast on her sixteenth
birthday. In the photograph, the star dancers are center stage, framed by the
corps de ballet. The costumes function as part of the spectacle and as signs of
gender and relative importance of the dancers. Photo © 1981 by Johan Elbers.

69. At this contact improvisation performance in 1984, the dancers, dressed
in gender-neutral casual clothes, focus on each other, not on an audience. The
shape formed by the bodies results from weight counterbalances rather than an
attempt to design a stage picture. The studio setting and background reinforce
the informal nature of the dancing. Photo © 1984 by Bill Arnold.

70. Arther Mitchell's Dance Theatre of Harlem performs "Les Biches," a revival of an early twentieth-century ballet choreographed in 1924 by Bronislava Nijinska (Vaslav Nijinsky's younger sister). An innovative ballet in many respects (and one which contains some unconventional partnering), it satirizes social manners in the '20s. It also follows a number of traditions, in part to heighten its satire: distinction between the movement styles of men and women; clothing which connotes character and gender roles; organization of space to provide a unified focal point for the viewer. Photo © 1983 by Johan Elbers.

71. Each dancer creates a focal point for the viewer in this contact improvisation class performance. Women and men move similarly in spherical pathways with an ongoing energy. Their clothing signifies informality and individual identity within a group conformity. Photo © 1985 by Bill Arnold.

usually sweatpants and T-shirts, tend to obscure the outline of the bodies. The bagginess and sometimes even padded quality of this clothing camouflage breasts, hips, and musculature, to some degree.[7]

Thus, a cluster of techniques of the body (Mauss 1973) exists which are associated with the sexual dimorphism and gender distinction of the ballet *pas de deux*. These techniques include outward presentation, control of space, strength and support for the male, and strength tempered by delicacy and dependence for the female. This cluster of techniques can also be associated with characteristics of the ballet as a social organization: the classification of ballet as a high art form and the hierarchical nature of ballet as it is taught in dance classes and as it is managed and performed in dance companies.

A contrasting cluster of techniques of the body which are associated with lack of gender distinction in contact improvisation includes the techniques of inward focus, disorientation and uncontrolled flow in space, and a combination of supporting and dependent movement for each and every dancer regardless of sex. This cluster can also be associated with the characteristics of contact improvisation as a social organization: the classification of contact improvisation as a "folk"-like dance and the egalitarian ideology of the form as it is practiced and taught. The delineation of these clusters does not fix any movement quality to a meaning, but it suggests how movement can become associated with a host of values which do not belong in the domain of dance alone but are also a part of how we understand our lives and see ourselves as male and female.

Cunningham Technique and Contact Improvisation

A second comparison of a movement style with contact improvisation illuminates other aspects of meaning. Merce Cunningham strongly influenced experimental dance, and Steve Paxton danced in his company in the early '60s. The continuities and differences in the two dance styles in terms of specific movements and choreographic traits help to clarify

7. Merce Cunningham offers a third example, somewhere between ballet and contact improvisation, of gender distinctions in movement and costume. In his company, men and women generally dress alike (or everyone dresses differently), and dancers are seldom assigned roles. Still, the men generally lift the women, partnering them in often unorthodox ways but partnering them (men manipulating the women) nonetheless. Cunningham's unisex costumes are also usually closely fitted leotards and tights, which tend to emphasize the physical differences of the male and female bodies even while they also somewhat neutralize the body.

the nature of that influence and raise questions about the conventions of informality and presentation in dance.

An extension of certain "informal" qualities in Cunningham's work is apparent in contact improvisation. Cunningham's dancers generally do not "play" to an audience, nor do they portray characters. They tend to execute movement in a tasklike manner, although because much of the movement style resembles ballet, the "tasks" often do not seem like everyday movement. Cunningham did introduce some pedestrian, or everyday, movements like walking and running into his choreography. He also created multifocused movement events which could be viewed in the round and which eliminated a hierarchical use of space within the choreography and, to a degree, among dancers.

However, striking differences in presentation between Cunningham and contact improvisation are also evident. The pedestrian walking in Cunningham's dances looks much more uniform, uplifted, and stiffly controlled, or "held," than the walking in contact improvisation. In part, this is because the Cunningham dancers are still "performing" consciously, paying attention to maintaining their aligned, vertical stance even while avoiding the dramatic presentation of traditional modern dance. The "neutral" stance of the Cunningham dancers is a sign that the person's movement itself, not the person as revealed by the movement, holds primary significance.

Contact improvisers, on the other hand, consciously cultivate a more "natural" stance, walking as they would walk down the street rather than performing a "dancer's walk"; this stance signifies that each person is different from every other and is just a person "being" or "behaving," not a person "performing." One might say that the Cunningham dancers treat pedestrian movement as they would a virtuoso leap, whereas contact improvisers treat a virtuoso leap as they would a pedestrian movement.[8]

The differences between Cunningham's walk and that of contact improvisers help identify the conventions which indicate naturalness in the period of American modern dance from the '50s to the early '80s. For Cunningham, as for Alwin Nikolais, the neutral stance differentiates the

8. This calling upon an everyday, American stance in contact improvisation and other "pedestrian" dancing makes for problems in cross-cultural transmission. In Japan, for example, not only are the strictures against public touching more prevalent, but also the "everyday" walk is more "held," controlled. Contact improviser Joan Laage, who has taught dance in Japan, said that the Japanese dancers attempting to do contact improvisation tend to be either too stiff, or, if told to "relax," go completely limp, "like puppets."

72. The Merce Cunningham Company in "Roratorio" (1986) stand and sit attentively. On the one hand, their activity is simple and pedestrian; on the other hand, it is performed deliberately, with bodies controlled and erect. Photo © 1986 by Johan Elbers.

73. Falling off balance, the implied trajectories of movement by these contact improvisers contrasts with the solid verticality of the dancers in illustrations 72 and 74. Photo © 1985 by Bill Arnold.

74. This photograph of the Merce Cunningham Company in "Sounddance" (1975) suggests an interesting combination of movement qualities. Karole Armitage, held aloft by Chris Komar, *left*, and Rob Remley, *right*, displays her classical ballet and modern dance technique and creates clear linear design. The men who support her are tasklike in their action, as is Louise Burns who has just walked through the passageway of bodies. Cunningham, *foreground*, gestures in a more rounded, idiosyncratic manner, seemingly unrelated to the other dancers. Photo © 1980 by Johan Elbers.

dancer from the dramatic character of traditional modern dance. For contact improvisers, focus on oneself and one's partner indicates an absorption in what is going on and differentiates the performer from any kind of presentational dancer.

For many experimental dancers during the '60s and '70s, inward focus was considered more natural; outward focus was seen to indicate a major concern with pleasing an audience,[9] with presenting an (artifi-

9. Yvonne Rainer wrote about her "Trio A" (1966) that "either the gaze was averted or the head was engaged in movement. The desired effect was a worklike rather than exhibitionlike presentation" (1974:67).

cial) image of oneself rather than the real, or authentic, self. Contact improvisation dancers and audiences also identified signs of naturalness like coughing, laughing, adjusting clothes, and so on, with "anti-elitism": the performer could be seen as just another person, not someone special and separate from the audience. To many, these conventions helped identify contact improvisation as a kind of contemporary folk dance. The theoretical counterpositions in the '60s and '70s of focus toward the self and focus toward the audience contrast with the sense of possible shared communication between performer and audience characteristic of earlier modern dance. In dance, as in other areas of American life, modernist faith in communicating solutions to large problems and expressing the human condition on a grand scale had seriously eroded. What had previously seemed noble now seemed pompous.

Response to performance conventions of the "natural" changed, not only from one audience to another, but also through time. Many viewers of Cunningham's and Nikolais' early work thought that the dancers were robotic, unfeeling, and inhuman because of their neutral facial expressions. When performances of this kind of work moved into mainstream theaters and were acclaimed as major American dance—as had happened with Graham—the ugly became beautiful. Experimental dance conventions—inward focus, dressing and behaving informally, using pedestrian movement—were at first a shock to and an assault on audience expectations. As audiences became more accustomed to these ideas, and as a range of choreographers played with them, their specific evocative quality was lessened and the formal character of the dance movement was emphasized. Eventually, these conventions of the natural in dance appeared in all sorts of performances, often unmoored from their original contexts; natural behavior could consciously be employed presentationally (as in Paul Taylor's "Esplanade" [1975]) or ironically (as in Twyla Tharp's "Push Comes to Shove" [1976]).

The differences between Cunningham technique and contact improvisation are even more marked in the area of movement styles.[10] Cunningham's style emphasizes space and time, with various body parts often moving simultaneously in different directions and the dancer focused outwardly; contact improvisation emphasizes weight and flow, with the body often moving in a segmented, successional fashion and the dancer focused inwardly. A Cunningham dancer "refers constantly to the verti-

10. Laban movement analyst Tara McClellan has interpreted contact improvisation as the antithesis of Cunningham technique in movement style (1980).

cal" while the periphery of the body—arms, legs, head—initiates movement and traces spokes and arcs through the space; a contact improviser falls off the vertical while the core of the body—pelvis, spine, shoulders —initiates movement and traces three-dimensional spirals through the space (McClellan 1980).[11]

The contrasts between Cunningham technique and contact improvisation also indicate larger cultural trends in movement style, not just differences in personal preference. Whereas Cunningham's movement style had been influenced significantly by other theater dance forms, notably Graham and the ballet style of George Balanchine, experimental dancers (including Paxton) in the '60s and '70s focused primarily outside of theater dance—on social dance, sport, physical theater, and pedestrian actions—for inspiration.

Contact Improvisation as Part of a Movement Environment

It seems evident that prominent aspects of the movement style of social dance in the '60s permeated the performance dance of the '70s. In the social dance of the '60s, the qualities of focusing inwardly while dancing and moving in an ongoing, freely flowing manner were part of what offended some Americans and pleased others about this social dance (see Chapter 2). These movement elements became associated with social ideas of freedom and individuality within an egalitarian collective. They also became part of the American movement environment, social facts in and of themselves, implicitly perceived and understood by everyone.[12] People moved in particular ways, generating feelings, often unarticulated, about the "right" way to live and to dance.

Theater director Peter Brook alludes to the changeable nature of movement, as well as its reality, when he writes about producing plays at Stratford, England:

> . . . about five years, we agree, is the most a particular staging can
> live. It is not only the hairstyles, costumes and make-ups that look

11. McClellan also suggests that the contrast between the two techniques indicates Paxton's logical recuperation in terms of movement after he left the Cunningham Company.

12. Leo Marx (1964) makes an analogous point about symbols in American literature. It is not enough, he suggests, "to sum up the 'ideas' embodied in the symbol if we are to appreciate its impact upon the serious writers of the age. For its meaning is carried not so much by express ideas as by the evocative quality of the language, by attitude and tone" (193).

dated. All the different elements of staging—the shorthands of behavior that stand for certain emotions . . . —are all fluctuating on
an invisible stock exchange all the time. Life is moving, influences
are playing on actor and audience, and other plays, other arts, the
cinema, television, current events, join in the constant rewriting of
history and the amending of the daily truth. (Brook 1968:16)

In this passage, Brook refers to movement as representation of particular
emotions. I am suggesting in addition that another reality exists in movement experience as well, a kinesthetic ambiance which helps to create
and which calls up the ethos and *mise en scène* of a particular time.

Each generation of modern dancers has claimed a new freedom, but
the style in which the freedom is embodied varies, and each generation
comes to accept its dance style as the "right" way to move. In a dance
genre like modern dance, which is innovative by definition, movement
styles change rather quickly, so allegiances to different forms coexist in

75. In this moment of Trisha Brown's "Opal Loop" (1980), the multifocused
nature of the movement is evident, as is the sense of ongoingness. Although
the choreography of this dance is predetermined and highly systematic, this
photograph could be taken to show four very interesting social dancers (*from left
to right,* Stephen Petronio, Eva Karczag, Lisa Kraus, and Trisha Brown). Photo
© 1980 by Johan Elbers.

the same time period. However, certain trends in movement can be observed. Contact improvisation has been a part of one of those trends, becoming a vehicle itself for the promulgation of movement ideas and of a movement environment.

In the early '70s, freely flowing movement, focus on the inner experience of moving, and energy thrown in all directions became very prevalent in American theater dance. These qualities appeared not just in contact improvisation, but also in the dances of choreographers such as Trisha Brown, Lucinda Childs, Laura Dean, and Twyla Tharp.

Tharp, for instance, who was consciously influenced by black dance and social dance traditions, developed a movement style which has been described by Billie Lepczyk as freely flowing and internally focused. These qualities, Lepczyk suggests, are "least pronounced in ballet and in most previous major modern dance styles"; they "create a loose, carefree, casual manner which makes the movement appear easy—as if anyone could do it" (1981:129–31). The movement style of social dance shaped

76. The dancers in Twyla Tharp's "Baker's Dozen" (1979) appear to be catapulted, their arms thrown in the air, their movement tossed off. As Tharp has continued to do greater amounts of work for ballet companies (in 1989, she served as an artistic associate of American Ballet Theatre), her movement style has tended to be more controlled, with larger, more extended leg and arm gestures. Photo © 1980 by Johan Elbers.

in the '6os and its implications—that it was loose, carefree, casual, and easy—continued into the '70s in theater dance.

Other events in the movement environment of the '70s signaled further changes. Disco dance, a popular dance form coinciding with contact improvisation, indicated different aesthetic and social interests. Whereas contact dancers partnered in any combination of male/male, female/male, or female/female, with both people free to give weight or to support at any time, disco dancers employed the traditional form of social-dance partnering in which the male led and directed the female. Disco dance was much more controlled than contact improvisation. It emphasized relating to a partner through sight and one-way manipulation instead of touch and mutual control.

Disco dancers transformed rock dancing's focus on the self as an individual within a group into a display of self in synchrony with a partner of the opposite sex. Their movement style was much more outwardly directed and presentational, posed, and controlled. Dancers tended to focus their energy in one direction at a time, often exclusively toward a partner.

The movement in disco dance, particularly as popularized in the mass media, encoded planning, control, and "straight" heterosexual activity to a much greater extent than did either rock dancing or contact improvisation. One has only to think of the dances and story of *Saturday Night Fever* for illustration: John Travolta's character uses his showy, aggressive dancing to create a sense of self which is strong, competitive, and sexy. He manipulates his partners physically and emotionally as he dances with them. He matures by realizing that he must exert some of that same control in his everyday life and make something of himself by leaving his working-class neighborhood in Brooklyn for the possibility of upward mobility in Manhattan. Disco dancing becomes a metaphor for life, but at the same time, it is a childish activity, best left behind. The aggressive "macho" image of the dance must be tamed, not so that he can become a liberated man, but so that he can succeed in the real world of money and fame. (In his next film, Travolta became a "real" dancer, on Broadway.)

Since the late '70s and early '8os, movement trends evident in disco dancing became even more prominent. The relaxation prized in the '6os and through the '70s in some middle-class communities gave way to "stress management," and "looseness" gave way to the achievement of "fitness." Dancers participated in and often articulated these changes.

Perhaps the most popular "dance form" of the '80s, aerobics, cannot be considered either a social dance form or a theater form, but a kind of sports training which purports to help a person (usually a woman) gain control over her body and look good. Aerobic dancing often focuses on self-control and on the appearance rather than the experience of the body and movement. The ever-growing popularity of sports also seems notable, for the movement qualities and structures utilized in sports activities, although varied from one game to another, inevitably involve control and competitiveness.

The startling surge of interest in the mid-'80s in professional wrestling, a cross between a sport and a performance form, contrasted ironically with the still-existing practice of contact improvisation. Like contact improvisers, professional wrestlers perform and collaborate as partners through touch, but they do so in order to simulate a violent competition, a "spectacle," Roland Barthes called it, which in America represents "a sort of mythological fight between Good and Evil" (1972:23).

Ideally, contact improvisers carry on what they see as the sincere and intimate dialogue of two people through the interaction of their bodies, cooperating with the laws of physics and evoking images of comradery, play, nurturing, sport, sex, and love. Wrestlers, too, must cooperate with the laws of physics, but the singular image they evoke is one of violation, violence, and spectacle. Wrestlers engage in an elaborate choreography, which they and their mass audiences know is fake but pretend is real. The pleasure of watching wrestling lies partly in the discrepancy between the brutality depicted, which the audience can passionately cheer, and the reality that no blood is spilled and the wrestlers are seldom seriously injured. Rather than representing an honest dialogue, movement here is a theatrical trick, an outward appearance. a conspiracy by the wrestlers with each other and the audience, which the savvy viewer can appreciate on more than one level.

Theater dancers have also articulated changes in recent years, opting in many cases for greater control and flashiness. It is not only younger choreographers like Michael Clark or Molissa Fenley who create these images. Even Martha Graham's company, with its Halston costumes and attention to body line and arabesques, seems more polished and visually spectacular. This is not to say that dancers consciously plan these changes; like all participants in a culture (to paraphrase Marx), they make their own dances, but within a set of rules they do not always personally create.

77. In the long history of tap dancing, which originated in the late nineteenth century, a multiplicity of styles have been practiced. Baseline features, though, are the constant attention to rhythm (the sound of the feet being as important as the visual image) and, by definition, to the flow and shift of weight through the feet. Often, as illustrated in this photograph of Maurice and Gregory Hines, 1982, the body stance is relaxed and inwardly focused and the movement is freely flowing within the structure of the rhythmic patterns and phrases. UPI/Bettmann Newsphotos.

78. John Travolta, in his famous pose from *Saturday Night Fever*, aggressively confronts the spectator while his partner, clearly subordinate, dances alongside him. Travolta represents the mass cultural image of disco dancing; however, it should be remembered that disco had many local manifestations (some of them in group, not couple, form) and ethnic and/or social-class identities. The Bettmann Archive.

79. Another dance form which emerged in the '70s was break dancing, a competitive social dance developed in largely black and Hispanic New York neighborhoods by adolescent boys. As the media discovered the phenomenon, break dancing faded rapidly as a street form and became a kind of theater dance. In this photograph of the First Greater Washington Break Dancing Competition in 1984, the movement of the Mighty Poppalots resembles contact improvisation's athleticism and gymnastic ability to use 360-degree space. The costuming, music, and presentation, however, point to different origins, aesthetics, and meanings; break dancing, among other things, is about adolescent male prowess and performance, black and Hispanic street culture, and the social/political commentary of the rap music which accompanies it. UPI/ Bettmann Newsphotos.

80. The hybrid form of aerobics adapts well to competition and presentation. Dancers in this Hollywood contest in 1984 combine running with Broadway jazz movement. Again, it should be noted that mass cultural images are not necessarily the same as local practices (see Kagan and Morse 1988); many women (and men) have experienced aerobics classes as sources of physical pleasure and sociability. UPI/Bettmann Newsphotos.

81. Larry "Pretty Boy" Sharpe twists the arm of wrestling opponent Antonio Inoke. UPI/Bettmann Newsphotos.

82. Siatome Sensue at an aikido demonstration throwing his partner, Richard Heckler. Note the spherical movement of the throw so evident in this photograph; also, compare the facial expression of Siatome Sensue with those of the wrestlers in illustration 81. Photo © 1989 by Jan Watson.

83. Bill T. Jones and Julie West in "Shared Distance" (1978). Photo © 1981 by Chris Harris.

For example, in 1985, choreographer Bill T. Jones, who practiced contact improvisation early in his career (1974–76), discussed reviving a duet he had made in 1978 called "Shared Distance" (see illustration 83). The dance had been created originally with Julie West, who had also trained extensively in contact improvisation and had very little other dance experience.

> Julie and I were both involved in this kind of natural, free-wheeling, raw look when I made the dance. Now I'm working with a different dancer with no contact background and trying to understand how to change or revise the dance. When I push her through space, we [Jones and Arnie Zane] keep saying, "Well, you should keep your legs together." Before, Julie would just come off flying. Why do we suddenly feel that that's not appropriate now, that when I push her away, she should look designed in the air?
>
> These things are very real. My past and my future meet in this piece, and I'm trying to understand it. "The messy look," "cleaning up the act"—contact was about messiness.

The sentiments of this choreographer *are* about very real things. How we move constitutes a part of our past and our future. The "free-wheeling, raw look" is not a fixed definition for the movement characteristics of free flow and multiply-directed energy, and neither is messiness (certainly the Polynesians, whose dance contains free flow and multiply-directed energy, do not define the movement in these ways). "Free-wheeling," "raw," and "messy" are descriptions which Americans applied to certain movement qualities in particular cultural and historical times. In 1978, Bill T. Jones saw free flow and indirectness as being natural and free-wheeling; in 1985, these same qualities signified messiness to him.

Many reasons exist for the diminishing performances of contact improvisation in the '80s, but certainly, the changes in the American movement environment were a contributing factor. The daily truth of movement was gradually amended, and contact improvisation no longer seemed quite as immediate and vital to some people as it once was.

6
Experiencing the Body

Conceptions and practices in American culture construct the body and its techniques; we learn what our bodies are and how to move them in all of our social interaction. Dance focuses on techniques of the body directly and extensively. Although sometimes viewed as sets of skills, dance techniques provide movement experiences, body images, and conceptions of body, self, and motion with far-reaching implications. Contact improvisation, as one American construction of the body and of ways in which the body can and should move, constitutes a commentary which is culturally revealing.

Learning Contact Improvisation

In the process of learning contact improvisation, a person acquires skill in a way of moving rather than in executing a particular set of moves. Learning this way of moving eventually involves interacting with another person, although the student sometimes uses the floor as the "partner" in beginning stages of practicing contact improvisation movement skills. Regardless of differences in approach from one teacher of contact improvisation to another, all teachers instruct their students to focus on the physical sensations of touch and the pressure of weight. Thus, in the learning process, the sense of touch and physical reflex actions assume more importance for the dancer than the sense of vision and consciously chosen actions.

When doing contact improvisation, the weight and height of another dancer do not indicate how easy or difficult it will be to dance with him or her. Contact improvisation does not rely on muscular strength, although strength may allow for the execution of certain movements. But because each dancer is supposed to do only what he or she is able, people of radically different sizes and weights can dance quite well together; the key to being a good partner rests on one's movement awareness within the parameters of the form.

In addition to sensitizing oneself to weight and touch, a student of contact improvisation must accept disorientation and learn to be turned upside down or sideways, moving through space in spiraling or curving motions rather than in the more usual axial motion of everyday action. At first, the sense of spatial disorientation cultivated in the form sometimes frightens people. To some degree, their fear stems from a reasonable reaction to physical danger. Especially during the early years of contact improvisation, the form really was dangerous because no one knew what might happen; dancers were trying to discover the possibilities for the action of two bodies flinging somewhat uncontrollably through space together. Students thus have needed to learn techniques of falling so that they can respond quickly and appropriately to surprising events and avoid injury. The edge of physical danger in contact improvisation has always been appealing and exciting to some people. Like many athletic activities, contact improvisation can offer the exhilaration of safely accomplishing dangerous feats.

The act of minimizing control can also carry frightening social implications. Disorientation in American social behavior is usually interpreted as a sign of mental instability, and lack of physical control is generally thought of as a sign of injury, illness, or intoxication.[1] Both ballet and modern dance traditions incorporate falling or freely flowing action within very strict spatial boundaries and controlled, choreographed phrases of movement. Contact improvisation is virtually the only contemporary American theater dance form that emphasizes the wildness and awkwardness of falling, relying on conditioned or reflexive controls and strategies rather than on choreographed movement. Experiencing contact improvisation can teach an enjoyment of disorientation and a reconsideration of spatial associations.

In the process of writing this book, I studied the techniques of contact improvisation by taking classes and by participating in jams and workshops. At the beginning of my study, I found my background as

1. See Murphy 1987 for a discussion of the stigma associated with disability, a stigma derived in part from the perception of lack of physical control as abnormal and even less than human.

a dancer of limited use to me when in contact with another person's weight. In a contact improvisation class taught by Randy Warshaw, I was encouraged to focus almost exclusively on sensing weight by lying on the floor with my eyes closed, feeling my own weight settle into the ground, becoming aware of the touch of my skin against the floor, and losing all track of time. As I started to experience an internalized sensation of moving, my image of what my movement looked like for an observer dropped away, and I became immersed in the feeling of tiny changes of weight and the smallest movement of my joints.

Settled in this state, when I came into contact with another dancer, I was intensely focused on moment-to-moment awareness of change. My sensitivity to touch and weight made me responsive to subtle shifts in my partner's actions. I then began to experience periods of an effortless flow of movement, not feeling passive, and yet not feeling actively in control either. The sensation of "being guided by the point of contact" with my partner fitted the description of "allowing the dance to happen" to me. The quality and mood of the dancing sometimes remained fairly constant during a duet, but more often fluctuated with the energy and phrasing of our movement. When the dance was over, I felt as if I had exerted my entire body, but without consciously working hard. If rapport had been established in the dance—that is, if the movement with my partner seemed fairly mutual in direction, momentum, and timing so that it felt as though the dance had moved us—I also experienced a strong sense of communion with my partner, even if I had never met him or her before.

Proceeding to study from a variety of teachers, I found that, although they used different approaches to "sensory" preparation, the development of internal awareness always constituted a part of class.[2] Through this work, I gained a better ability to concentrate and focus on weight and touch; at the same time, by practicing the form, I could feel that my body was also becoming trained in the spiraling pathways which contribute to an ongoing flow of movement of two bodies in contact. The experience differed from any I had had before in dancing.

My efforts to learn sometimes led me to attempt to control the movement, to make events occur. I discovered that unless a skill was really "in my body," a part of my movement repertoire that could emerge or

2. The use of extensive floor work to teach the sensory state necessary to do contact improvisation was developed in "the second wave" of contact improvisation, not in the form as it was initially taught, often on mats, during 1972–74.

be called on when appropriate, I would lapse into an awkward state of manipulating my own movement or my partner's. If I or my partner became consciously manipulative, the dance seemed frustrating. On the other hand, concentrating entirely on sensation produced a very limited kind of contact improvisation, instructive and fascinating to practice, but finally a bit monotonous and without dynamic range. I began to understand that the technique of doing contact improvisation takes time and much practice to absorb and that a dialogue exists between sensations of activity and receptivity.

If the most basic skills in contact improvisation are cultivating a state of awareness of weight and touch and learning to be disoriented, many more skills follow from that state when interacting with another person. All contact improvisers practice certain kinds of movement: falling, rolling, inverting, supporting weight with different body parts, being supported, yielding and softening the body, and using peripheral vision

84. The Pilobolus Dance Theatre in "Day Two" (1980). This company, which began in the early '70s, became famous for its use of gymnastic movement; it shares with contact improvisation a conception of 360-degree space. However, Pilobolus performs set choreography with movement that tends to be single-focused, controlled, oriented towards shaping the body and the space outside the body, and consciously choreographic; contact improvisation, which is generated as the dance occurs, tends to be multifocused, freely flowing, oriented towards internal body changes, and not consciously choreographic. Thus, the quality of movement and the "look" and kinesthetic sensation of Pilobolus' dancing differ markedly from contact improvisation. Photo © 1980 by Clemens Kalischer.

85. Kirsten Wilson and Pam Schwartzberg practice "surfing," an exercise in weight exchange. One person rolls perpendicularly over her partner; as she slides onto the floor, the roles are reversed and the partner "takes a ride." Photo © 1988 by Darlene Weide.

so that the eyes have a wide and general, rather than direct and specific, focus. Some teachers have students practice particular skills as a way of establishing habits of movement which might then be utilized in dancing; others teach the state of awareness they think the form requires and simply let people dance and test movement in the process. In either case, direction by the teacher seldom involves presentation of a movement to be copied precisely. Rather, the students attempt a particular kind of movement with different people and learn through doing it how to adjust for different bodies and how to gauge the possibilities for continuing movement sequences through their contact with each other.

At different points in the history of the development of contact improvisation, teachers have stressed different qualities. Whereas contact improvisation in the early '70s had been risky to perform, a raw and emotional experience because of its unpredictability, emphasis on flow and facility in movement skills in the late '70s and early '80s encouraged dancing that was often extremely smooth, controlled, and continuous. A

86. Two couples, one standing on the floor (Nancy Ryszewski and Nancy Stark Smith) and the other (unidentified) balanced behind them on a ballet barre, practice dancing "head to head," sensitizing themselves to the movement that might result from this mutual contact. Photo © 1984 by Jack Orton.

87. The sense of touch supports synchrony of motion as Cathy Jenkins and Margery Stamper fall into a run during their improvisation. Photo © 1988 by Darlene Weide.

88. Students lie next to each other, waiting to balance someone on hands and feet. As well as being an exercise in giving and receiving weight, this activity places students in a position of mutual responsibility for each other. Photo © 1985 by Lou Danielson Stewart.

89. Students at the School for American Ballet stand equidistant in a rect-
angular grid, facing the teacher and the mirror, each dancer separate in space
but moving in unison with others, practicing precision of her or his own body
placement in space. Photo © 1979 by Johan Elbers.

number of contact improvisers saw that period of smoothness as a stage
that by the mid-'80s was being countered by an interest in conflict, in
being surprising and not doing the expected action, and in incorporating
elements like eye and hand contact purposely omitted from the form as
it is usually initially taught and as it was initially developed.

**Sensuousness and Sexuality:
The Image and Experience of Touch**

For both practitioners and viewers, contact improvisation cultivates a particular kind of sensual involvement as a result of its focus on two bodies
moving together through the exchange of weight. In theory, all theater
dance engages sensuous response in the viewer. As an art form, it seeks
to provide aesthetic pleasure through appeal to the senses, the mind, and

90. Three simultaneous duets are occurring in this contact improvisation class (Caroline Palmer and Pam Schwartzberg, *foreground*), each one independently exploring different relationships of touch, weight, and momentum. Photo © 1988 by Darlene Weide.

the emotions. To a greater degree than visual art or music, dance (and, often, theater) appeals to the sense of touch and to the kinesthetic sense (the perception of movement in the body) as well as to vision and hearing. How those sensuous activities are perceived and interpreted, however, remains selective and particular to the performers, the choreography, and the audience as people learn about the meaning of the movement through doing and watching it.

In America, one body touching another body is highly charged with meaning and appropriate only in specific contexts. Edward T. Hall, who has studied attitudes towards distance between people and its cultural implications, defines "intimate distance" (ranging from actual touch to a separation of about eighteen inches) for middle-class Americans as the "distance of lovemaking and wrestling, comforting and protecting" (Hall 1969:117). Everyday social comportment (the handshake), confrontation in sport, touching in sexual interaction, and nurturing of children by parents (and, by extension, of one friend by another and of the injured or ill by health-care workers) constitute major activities in which touch is acceptable in American culture. Dance constitutes another, less commonly discussed, activity; contact improvisation presents a unique situation within dance.

Comparing the interaction between dancers in ballet and those in contact improvisation highlights differences of interpreting touch and images of the body. Ballet, which emphasizes female/male dimorphism, most often presents the two dancers in a representation of real social encounter, even when the two characters are mythical—a prince and a swan, for example. The concept of social encounter is suggested not only by the frequent narrative content of ballet, but also by the techniques of the body. A great deal of touching and gesture involves eye focus, facial expressions, and arm and hand motions, and the glances and gesticulations of the performers have meanings which can be socially decoded, often as a message of romantic love—"I love you," "I want you but I can't have you," "Please help me," "I'm angry," and so on. At the same time, the meanings of these gestures become reinforced by their use in the context of the ballet (see illustration 91).

Ballet also incorporates touching and body contact which operate as function and design so that the man can lift and maneuver the woman and the woman can be partnered in visually attractive ways. In this case, both the characters in the performance and the audience have learned that touching is part of the convention of executing the *pas de deux* and part of the visual abstract design of the choreography (see illustration 92). Social or sexual meanings are not meant to be explicitly read into these gestures, although the general meaning of the ballet may invest the encounter with sexual undertones. The man's hand on the woman's inner

91. The facial expressions and arm gestures of Carla Fracci and Erik Bruhn, dancing the lead roles in "Romeo and Juliet," signify the feelings of the lovers in the story. Photo 1967, UPI/Bettmann Newsphotos.

92. Maria Bylova and Leonid Nikonov rehearse for a performance of the
Bolshoi Ballet Company in London, 1986. UPI/Bettmann Newsphotos.

thigh, even in a love scene, rarely caresses but rather steadies or lifts his partner; the audience almost certainly finds an erotic content to the *pas de deux* on a metaphoric level, but like strangers pressed body to body in a crowded subway car, almost no one mistakes these techniques of the body for sexual acts.[3]

In contact improvisation, the functional use of touching predominates. The form depends on communication between dancers through the sense of touch and weight. Dancers use sight peripherally, not in eye contact; in fact, they seldom encounter each other face to face. The arms, legs, torso, even head, all provide potential surfaces for support or for contact. Those parts normally considered social and expressive in American culture—the head, the arms, the hands—are used as levers and as physical mass, thus distancing them from the emotional or symbolic meanings they might automatically carry in other dance forms. Likewise, parts of the body normally considered of sexual significance, taboo to touch in public, are to some degree desexualized by their use in the dance.

Interestingly, contact improvisers sometimes engage in actions which resemble love-making, yet their dancing can appear less erotic than the ballet, which incorporates social and emotional gesture (and often narrative) concerning love and desire. Contact improvisation, which posits as its central technique the physical encounter between two bodies considered as weight and mass, usually conveys sensuality. But its construction of the body as not gendered enables perception of interactions as not sexual (see illustration 93).

Of course, contact improvisation can have sexual or emotional content invested in it through the interpretation of an observer or by the presentation of the performers. One of the ways in which contact improvisation contains humor or poignancy in performance is through the sudden appearance and mutual recognition by the dancers and audience of a socially meaningful gesture: a crotch hold, for instance, may be laughingly recognized as a taboo action by the dancers and the audience

3. This analogy between touch in dance and touch in the subway holds true only in that a convention is observed in both cases. In dance, however, as opposed to subway riding, the touching usually is perfectly acceptable to everyone involved; it is merely perceived and interpreted in a specific way. In a crowded subway, as Edward Hall (1969) has noted, people try to ignore the fact that touching is occurring, removing the intimacy of contact by being "as immobile as possible" and keeping the muscles in the contact area tense. In addition, "the eyes are fixed on infinity and are not brought to bear on anyone for more than a passing glance" (118).

93. Peter Bingham seems to hold Andrew Harwood as if he were carrying any kind of object. The dancing which preceded and followed this moment may have given it specific implications, however, for the spectators who witnessed it. Photo © by Chris Randle.

laughs in response, or a cradling movement becomes intentionally sustained and the tenderness of the moment is emphasized (see illustrations 94 and 95).

On a more subtle but even more important level, sexuality becomes one of many personal physical and emotional sensations which viewers can read in a performer. Contact improviser John LeFan commented on this complexity: "The best dancing in contact improvisation is when people find a balance between who they are and the dancing. . . . Sexuality is there but it's treated like anything else, not like the big 'S.' Because of that, it's beautiful to see it come and go."

The sexual ambiguity inherent in the structure of contact improvisation affects practitioners as well as viewers. Teachers, particularly in the early years of development of the form, cautioned students about becoming involved in what Steve Paxton called "the gland game" while

94. Dena Davida catches Daniel Godbout in "Each Man for Herself" (1988). The resemblance between this catch and an embrace suggests social meanings in the dance. Photo by Normand Grégoire. Courtesy of Dena Davida.

trying to do contact improvisation. They warned that focus on sexual encounter or psychological interaction rather than on touch and weight as the impetus for generating movement could be physically dangerous for the partners, as well as stifling to the development of the dance. Since the dance form demands concentration on touch as a signal for how the two bodies are moving together, distraction from that focus risks one's own or another's safety. Although the teaching emphasizes inner sensation rather than visual experience of one's own movement, an orientation which bears more similarity to '60s social dance than to other perfor-

95. In 1981, Robin Feld choreographed "Parlor Dance." She developed it from contact improvisation and used a couch as a prop. The presence of this social object as the context for the body contact made the dance extremely funny and suggestive. Luc Petton, *above*, and Ariella Vidach. Photo © 1981 by Jack Jaeger.

mance forms, that awareness must be balanced by an alert stance towards the partner's movement and the environment.

Several contact improvisers, when the subject of touching was raised, related the origins of contact improvisation to the atmosphere of the early '70s, the "touchy-feely, group encounter" era. Undoubtedly, the popularity of encounter groups, transactional psychology, and general sexual experimentation among young people in the early '70s contributed to the acceptance of contact improvisation. Clear parallels exist between the format of the encounter group and that of contact improvisation, the former emphasizing honest dialogue between people talking, the latter, between people moving. If members of encounter groups were searching for an interactive experience which depended on "honesty" and "spontaneity," contact improvisers were doing the same in the realm of dance (Egan 1971; Graff 1985).

At the same time, Steve Paxton's association of touch with biomechanics and gravity ideologically separated the dance form from direct psychological and sexual encounter. "What always struck me about contact," said writer Elizabeth Zimmer, "was that it had the rigor of a dance

96. In a 1973 performance, this audience of college students collapsed together at the end of Anna Halprin's "Trance Dance" (1971). The interest of so many college students in an event like this was not unusual during the late '60s and early '70s. Courtesy of Anna Halprin.

form and was yielding me the same kind of self-insight that all that talking and all those encounter groups did." Mark Russell, originally an actor, had been attracted to "physical theater work" in college but had been discouraged by the tendency for actors to turn touching exercises into "group grope." "When I started studying contact improvisation," he said, "the dance form really clicked for me because it was sensual but not sexual. It was clear, the rules were strong. . . . Emotional things could come out, but they didn't have to, and you still got the pleasure of holding someone, carrying someone. . . ."

Ellen Elias offered two stories that illustrate the ways in which rules and social context define the interpretation of movement. She recalled teaching a class which only one student, a male beginner, attended. Elias and her student soon began to feel awkward doing rolling exercises together, and Elias became a bit fearful that sexual encounter would develop. "It taught me about context," she said. "Contact is intimate, but it is public; you need other people there for legitimacy, for reinforcing the set of values connected to doing the form." Without the presence of a class and teacher emphasizing touch as a means of generating the dance, the social, sexual aspects of touching became too predominant.

Elias also remembered a class taught in New York City by John LeFan in which the students practiced naming the body parts of the point of contact between partners in order to increase physical awareness. While all the students were saying phrases like "knee-hip," "chest-shoulder-head," one man began shouting out "breasts, thighs, breasts." "It was really awful—totally inappropriate," recalled Elias, "and it made me realize how appropriately everyone usually behaved."

In my interviews and conversations, dancers ranging from beginning level to the most experienced discussed the implications of touching and weight-bearing that are inherent in contact improvisation. They often related touching to a freedom from the restrictions of gender roles and from accompanying expectations about what kind of movement suits men and women and what parts of the body can and cannot be touched. Dancers felt that contact improvisation allows for partners to engage in close physical contact without necessarily experiencing sexual feelings and to engage in movement uncharacteristic of gender roles.

"Contact improvisation has redefined a woman's strength capacities and possibilities and a man's sensitivity," said Silvy Panet-Raymond, a Canadian contact improviser. "It has also changed the quality of the touch in dance . . . a hand gesture used to have an emotional charge or form a linear design. Now, it is not just presentational or expressive, it is supportive." Many women say they believe contact improvisation has offered them the opportunity to feel strong and to experience physical trust from men.[4] Many men feel contact improvisation has enabled them to experience physical contact with both women and men that is neither confrontational (as in largely male contact sports like wrestling or football) nor sexual.

One former amateur boxer and athlete who was learning contact

4. Kris Wheeler, a dancer and teacher from Seattle, said that she was so concerned with being identified as a strong woman that, for a time in the '70s, she deliberately danced with the largest men in the room in any class or jam. She ended up with a back injury. Wheeler's case is an exception, however. Many relatively smaller women and men have done contact improvisation successfully for years (as Wheeler has since her recovery) with women and men larger than they.

97. Alan Ptashek and Bruce Curtis, of the Exposed to Gravity Project. Photo © 1987 by Danielle Haim.

98. Marsha Paludan, *above,* and Robin Gilmore, of Creative Association. Photo © 1986 by Gary Mackender.

improvisation suggested that contact "puts you in touch with something experienced as a child with parents—it's a nurturing kind of dance." Dancers commented that they often feel protective or caring towards their partners, even when the partner is someone they do not know. "Contact improvisation has been successful because it feels good," one dancer said. "It's fun, healing, sensuous, and playful." For participants not involved in performance, these elements are particularly important, because they encourage social and therapeutic experiences of the dance form.[5]

Many dancers also experience a sensuality in doing contact improvisation which is particularly enjoyable because it is *not* explicitly sexual and therefore does not present sexual problems. "I feel lucky to have fallen into this dance form," said Danny Lepkoff, "and to have all this backlog of touching other people. It just doesn't happen for people who don't do contact. And I enjoy being able to dance with men without

5. Although the therapeutic effects of contact improvisation have always been appreciated, its uses as a tool for therapy emerged to a greater extent in the mid-'80s. In England, where contact improvisation was joined with release technique to a large degree, it did become widely used in transactional psychological therapy in the '70s.

99. Karen Nelson and Andrew Harwood. Photo © 1986 by Bill Arnold.

being homosexual, or even dealing with that issue at all." One man, who had done no dancing before, said that his first experiences doing contact improvisation were overwhelmingly emotional. They were the first times he had touched another man, except to shake hands or put an arm around a shoulder, since he had been a child. Similarly, several men who are gay commented that contact improvisation had allowed them unique experiences of (nonsexual) intimacy with both women and men.

The sensuality of contact improvisation is connected not only with the sense of touch but also to some degree with smell. General protocol among contact improvisers, as among most American dancers, is that one is washed and wears clean clothes for any dance session. But in the course of dancing, the smell of bodies, especially that of a partner, becomes one of many physical sensations inherent in dancing. A few contact improvisers mentioned this experience as a part of the pleasure of the dancing.[6]

Several people I talked to thought that sexual encounter might be more likely for people doing contact improvisation than other dance forms. Gurney Bolster, for example, felt that sexuality is raised within the dance form itself and, "while often downplayed, it can be taken advantage of. . . . By letting down social barriers, you're becoming vulnerable." Bolster pointed to potentially disturbing possibilities, but Kris Wheeler suggested that many young dancers "coming of age sexually" have found contact improvisation "a beautiful context for sexual exploration." On the other hand, Peter Ryan thought there is some danger inherent in constantly treating another body as if it were the floor—"it starts to feel just like the floor, like an impersonal object." On balance, most dancers thought that contact improvisation does not become a vehicle for sexual encounter to any greater extent than other dance forms or other kinds of social activity, for that matter.

Alternative to the circumstances and meanings of touching in American culture, the interpretations of touch offered by contact improvisation allow participants the possibility of constituting the body and self differently; the difficulties of this reconstitution point to the extent of dominant conceptions of the body in American culture. The debate over

6. When I started doing contact improvisation, several dancer friends who had never studied it joked about my "rolling around with all those unwashed strangers." Perhaps their jokes were connected with stereotypes from the '60s (unwashed hippies); perhaps they were simply reactions to breaking the taboo on casual physical intimacy, something that occurs to a greater degree in contact improvisation than in many other kinds of dancing.

100. Julyen Hamilton and Danny Lepkoff. Photo © 1985 by Bill Arnold.

sexuality versus sensuality in contact improvisation, although not resolvable, offers strong testimony to the power of cultural definition in influencing perceptions of sexuality.

Evaluations of the Dancing

If internal awareness and responsiveness to another characterize the body in contact improvisation, how might a contact improviser evaluate such skills, both his or her own and those of others? Like the martial art of aikido, contact improvisation has most often been taught "dojo" style, in classes with people of varying amounts of experience, avoiding formal delineations of "level." Unlike aikido, teachers do not award "belts" or any other kind of formal symbol signifying achievement of a level of skill. Yet definitions of skill have emerged and ways of acknowledging skill exist.

Particularly in the early days of contact improvisation, dancers claimed to view the form as "no-fault dancing." Dancers were theoretically "released from judgement," from the burden of having mastered or not mastered something. The major concern was simply to have an experience with movement and with other people. Here again, contact improvisation differs from martial art and more closely resembles social dancing.

Even in the early performances, the presentation aimed to demonstrate a dance form rather than to achieve a particular conception of a dance. According to Lisa Nelson, evaluation consisted of talking about how long it took "to get into it," that is, to cease moving tentatively; it also consisted of noticing, as a matter of interest, who danced with whom. Performers felt some obligation to observe the egalitarian decorum of dancing with as many people as possible and, for the sake of showing the work to an audience, to insure that there was at least one duet each of man with man, woman with woman, and woman with man. Yet they displayed little concern with the overall shaping of the concert, and, although a particularly risky physical occurrence or profoundly emotional moment might be mentioned and discussed,[7] they tended not to worry about judging what had transpired.

As people became more practiced at doing the form and the number of performances increased, other kinds of evaluation of performances

---

7. Discussing emotional moments indicates a valued aspect of even the earliest dancing, at least among some people, which was not formally emphasized in training.

101. Helen Clarke and Peter Bingham of the dance group Fulcrum. Photo ©
1978 by Chris Randle.

began to develop; simultaneously, dancers' desire and ability to shape a
concert increased. These developments led to making certain differen-
tiations between skilled and less skilled, and eventually between amateur
and professional. However, in the practice of the form, in classes and at
jams, participants drew no public, explicit distinction between experienced and inexperienced dancers for a number of years. Even in current
practice, most people accept that some partners are easier to dance with
than others, but they also accept the ethos that a person should be free
to dance with anyone and that nobody should be left out.

  Thus, the dancer new to contact improvisation at any time could
fairly quickly consider himself or herself a part of the group, and more
experienced contact improvisers often felt not just obligated to dance
with people less skilled than they, but also, in many cases, committed to
doing so. Some dancers told me that they believe the ability to dance with
anyone characterizes an advanced improviser, and they take seriously the
notion that, since contact improvisation concerns the physical dialogue

102. Contact improvisation has been taught and practiced in a wide range of populations, including disabled people. Alan Ptashek and Bruce Curtis, a man with spinal cord injury (SCI), have been dancing together since 1986, offering lecture-demonstrations and workshops under the name Exposed to Gravity Project. Kevin Finnan and Louis Richards of England and Karen Nelson and Alito Alessi of Seattle have organized workshops for disabled and able-bodied people to dance together. See *Contact Quarterly* 13 (Fall 1988). Photo © 1988 by Danielle Haim.

103. Alan Ptashek and Bruce Curtis. Photo © 1988 by Danielle Haim.

104. Bruce Curtis and Alan Ptashek. Photo © 1988 by Danielle Haim.

between two dancers, every dance presents a unique challenge. In practice, I found that teachers were the most generous about dancing with the less skilled; other dancers tended to seek partners on their own level or on a more advanced level than themselves (and, as a student myself, I had similar impulses).

The atmosphere of cooperation and mutual support cultivated in contact improvisation settings has encouraged many people reluctant to study other dance forms to try doing contact improvisation. Arnie Zane, interviewed in 1985, remembered that in 1973, he quickly forgot his self-consciousness at his very first dance class, a contact improvisation workshop.

> The people who were teaching it [Lois Welk, joined at some sessions by Jill Becker] had a real sense of freedom. They were not the dance world that I was so afraid of—actually the dance world I'm working with a lot now—but they were very open, nonthreatening . . . contact allowed me to dance. It said, "Okay, the body you have is fine. You can't do anything wrong once you get on the floor."

The concept of "no-fault dancing" and the minimizing of levels of achievement in explicit terms duplicates the atmosphere of many social dance situations and stands counterposed to virtually all modern dance and ballet teaching, even that of amateurs. This contrast points to one of the qualifications of an "art" dance or performance form in American culture: the dancing always includes an explicit judgement of skill level and ability. This characteristic separates performance from social dance, in which everyone should be able to participate.

The minimizing of public evaluation in contact improvisation also contributes to the wide range of "acceptable bodies" able to engage in the dance form. The varieties of height and weight among people skilled in contact improvisation contrast with the uniformities of height and weight among skilled performers in other dance forms, where narrow standards of both size and beauty are prevalent. The ideology of contact improvisation defines the self in terms of the action and sensation of the body rather than on the basis of the appearance of the body to other people, and it promotes a tolerance for a range of abilities and kinds of bodies.

7
Cultural Symbols
and Aesthetic Practices

Anthropologist David Schneider, in his classic study of American kinship, describes attitudes toward nature and the natural in American culture. Schneider argues that, although generally in American culture, "man's fate is seen as one which follows the injunction, Master Nature!," things are different "at home":

> Where kinship and family are concerned, American culture appears to turn things topsy-turvy. For this is one part of nature with which man has made his peace and in terms of which he is content to find his fate. What is out there in nature, say the definitions of American culture, is what kinship is. Kinship is the blood relationship, the fact of shared biogenetic substance. Kinship is the mother's bond of flesh and blood with her child, and her maternal instinct is her love for it. This is nature; these are natural things; these are the ways of nature. To be otherwise is unnatural, artificial, contrary to nature. (1980:107)

Schneider adds that what are considered the bad parts of nature in kinship, unregulated sexuality for example, are governed by the order of law. That order of law is predicated upon man's cultural attribute, reason, brought to bear on what is considered the good part of nature, the natural order of the family. "It is the order of law, based on reason and on nature, which, combined with nature, is the most powerful and the most nearly ideal arrangement in the definition of American culture" (1980:110).

Schneider's description of kinship parallels contact improviser Emily Ransom's description of dancing:

> Contact is a movement form that feeds into the positive, balanced, reasonable side of human nature but does not deny the daemonic. It gives permission for deep sensitivity but balances that with the ultimate realities of physical laws—gravity, momentum, inertia. Playing with this balance, it constantly self corrects the wrong moves and reinforces the right ones bringing forth a physical-emotional truth about a shared moment of movement that leaves the participants informed, centered and enlivened. (*Contact Quarterly* 2[Winter 1976]:16)

While Ransom's statement is undoubtedly an idealization, a summary of values as she interprets them, Schneider's description of kinship is also about the realm of values, what he calls the "cultural domain." Nature in contact improvisation is (ideally) like nature in the American home —powerful, truthful, connected with feelings of love and sharing with others which result from listening to and obeying the natural order of things. Within this "safe" context, wild, spontaneous events can occur. Human regulation exists in order to allow the dance to happen, not in order to impose itself on the truth of the dance.

That these views of nature in movement are both culturally and historically specific is clear from a cross-cultural example. Nature in the Balinese cosmology offers a graphic contrast to nature in American culture. In Bali, people conceive of human beings as suspended between two poles—one, the earth and sea (nature—residence of evil spirits), the other, the sky (residence of the good spirits). "Culture" in the Balinese construct provides the means of protection against the potential evils of the natural world; the vertical stance signifies order and control. A Balinese woman who fell down and broke her arm, reported Jane Belo, caused more concern because she fell down than because she was injured; a Balinese child watching American Ana Daniel stand on her head thought Daniel "a little crazy" to toy with evil spirits by inverting herself (Belo 1970:90; Daniel 1981:xvi–xvii). Contact improvisation could not mean the same things in Bali as in America.

Contact improvisation demonstrates and teaches American cultural values, sometimes reinforcing dominant ideas (the view of nature), at other times suggesting a response or alternative to dominant ideas (sense of touch, male and female roles). The concepts of the responsive body and the process of improvisation constitute cultural symbols enacted in the aesthetic practice of contact improvisation.

Physical Necessity

During the early development of contact improvisation, participants and teachers seldom explicitly discussed the need to define a form and maintain control over the improvisation. The most prominent features discussed seem to have been, first, physical necessity and, second, individual movement impulse in response to that necessity. In fact, the aesthetic of contact improvisation was largely conceived of as an appreciation of movement based on "survival," and on the "natural" and "honest" outcome of playing with weight, momentum, and gravity, an implied contrast to more "artificial, contrived" dance forms based on ideas or aesthetic concepts.

In 1984, Nancy Stark Smith described contact improvisation in an interview, relating the dance to the "honest, physical necessity" of moving and allowing movement to be guided by natural forces:

> The giving and sharing of weight sets up a kind of template. You can't lie about that stuff; you can't fake anything. There's a kind of directness in relationship to your body as a physical entity—you have weight, you have a skeleton, and, if you arrange it properly, it will be easier to move. You're putting your body on the line, and there's some risk involved, some awareness of safety, and contact with the forces of gravity and momentum—feeling them, really feeling them, feeling totally swept over by them. Something I've been really emphasizing the last couple of years is disorientation, experiencing spherical space, getting lost in the forces.

Smith's remarks recall Martha Graham's famous admonition that "movement never lies." Of course, Graham spoke of a psychological reality underlying movement; Smith spoke of a physical reality. Smith's comments also suggest that this physical reality reveals what is natural and true.

Many contact improvisation teachers and dancers stressed the concepts of relaxation and responsiveness and the intelligent characteristics of the body. Peter Ryan suggested that contact improvisation shows you the "difference between your real body and your idealized body" by asking what your body can do, not what you can make it do. Emphasis, he said, lies on "let, allow, release" rather than on "get, achieve, take, put." With contact improvisation, said David Woodberry, the instincts take over: "The body knows how to protect itself, because the body thinks faster than the mind." "As long as I stick to what is physically tangible," Randy Warshaw told a class, "it's okay. . . . When I go off into other areas, which people want to talk about all the time, it becomes distracting. Contact improvisation may provoke those things, but it's not the work."

Rather than any verbal instructions, creative or aesthetic ideas, or willed initiative on the part of the dancers, it is the physical laws which govern contact improvisation that were repeatedly mentioned in my interviews and in early issues of the *Newsletter* and in the *Quarterly*. Nature and natural movement were conceived of as supports for the unfolding of the dance, which happens to the partners if they allow it. Written material prior to the mid-'80s also tended not to stress creative or deliberate action.

In more extended discussions of contact improvisation with dancers and teachers, the fact that realizing the dance form requires active initiations as well as passive responses became evident. Any student of contact improvisation also learns quickly that, although one cannot just manipulate a partner, "allowing the dance to happen" does not mean that the dancers simply do nothing. An article written in 1975 by Steve Paxton for *The Drama Review* contains one of the clearest explanations of the idea which originally underlay "doing contact." Paxton, after stating that contact improvisation "as a social system" comprises different combinations of the elements active (A), passive (P), demand (d), and response (r), continues with the following description:

> One [person] may lift the other (Ad & Pr) [active demand and passive response]. One may fall so the other must catch (Pd & Ar) [passive demand and active response]. One may attempt to lift and find the energy translated so s/he is lifted (Ad & Ar) [active demand and active response], etc. But this all has to do with intent, which should be minimal, and the sensing of intent, which should be maximal. The more the forms are understood, the more cooperation becomes the subject—an "it" defined by the balancing of the inertias, momentums, psychologies, spirits of the partners. (1975:41)

Paxton's language, even as it acknowledges the activity of the partners, stresses sensing and responding to the "it," the third force that becomes created by the cooperation and interaction of two people. The underlying meaning of the "it" derives in part from belief in the rule of physical law and the connection of the body to nature, and in part from conceptions of the dynamics of improvisation in general and the particular use of improvisation in contact.

Physical Law and Nature

Contact improvisers are dealing with a particular and complex formulation of the physical, not only in the actual doing of the dancing but also in the ways in which people talk about and conceive of dancing. Language and movement are not synonymous, but they affect and inform each other. The notions of "natural laws" and of "meditating on them," of "sharing information through the body," and of the body "thinking faster than the mind" have important ramifications for the dancer's sense of self and for the relationships of nature and culture implicitly experienced in doing and watching the dance form.

The conception of the physical in contact improvisation has its roots in a number of sources, one of which was the emphasis by experimental dancers in the '50s and '60s on the moving body as the subject matter of the dance. Works in the classic modern dance tradition had represented the physical as the outward manifestation of the mind or of an inner, psychic reality, whereas much of the dance which followed it represented the physical as synonymous with the person, or at least with the dancer—what you see is what is, so to speak. For Merce Cunningham, for example, the physical did not symbolize anything from the performer's point of view; what the audience chose to perceive or interpret was left to the discretion and predilection of each viewer. For Erick Hawkins, Alwin Nikolais, and to some extent, Anna Halprin, the sensuous apprehension of the physical self by the dancer signaled the complete realization of movement; specific emotional messages need not be consciously conveyed.

The notion of allowing events to unfold in the way in which they are seen to occur in nature characterizes Zen Buddhist philosophy, which contributed to these artistic conceptions of the body. Since the '50s, Eastern philosophies have been of particular interest to many American intellectuals and artists, often because they have seemed to offer an alternative to existing European and North American models of art. By the '60s, Zen conceptions of acceptance of nature rather than mastery over it also coincided with some people's rejection of America's ecological attitudes and political policies. Zen was seen as an antidote to competitive striving and struggling, characteristic of capitalist society.

Aikido, the Japanese martial art which so influenced Steve Paxton, demonstrates Zen philosophy in its practice. Aikido is taught by a master who guides students in a series of physical experiences over many years, experiences which are thought to embody spiritual truths and values. In aikido, willful action, trying too hard to do something, is considered an interference with the natural manifestation of ki, the source of energy in the universe: "'The resonance of the body derives from the unity of mind and body which harmonizes with the resonance of the universe. The mutual response and interchange produces the ki of ai-ki'" (Master Ueshiba Morihei, founder of aikido, quoted in Ueshiba 1984:75).

Only by allowing the body to follow its protective reflexes (a natural response), in tune with the universe, and by retraining its impulses to tense and allow thoughts to control the movement (worldly and unnatural responses) can the martial art be practiced. "You have a much too willful will," the Zen master tells his frustrated archery student, Eugen Herrigel, in a book that helped to popularize Zen in America. "You think that what you do not do yourself does not happen" (Herrigel 1953:51). Particularly in the early years of contact improvisation, one can see how closely people modeled the form after principles of Eastern martial arts training.

The image of the body in contact improvisation combines the '60s modern dance conceptions of the body as synonymous with the person and movement as a sensuously apprehended experience with the Zen/aikido image of the body as responsive and intelligent, acting best and most correctly with the least amount of conscious will or intention possible. Paxton and his colleagues derived the structure or form of contact improvisation, but they allowed for large amounts of individual interpretation and realization. To a significant degree, the dance form replaced the director/choreographer who tells dancers what to do in order to create a work of art. The form itself became viewed simultaneously as the teacher, the master, and the choreographer; art does not imitate nature, in this case, it *is* nature.[1]

1. At the same time, the martial intent of aikido's physical interaction was replaced by notions of communicating to a partner and an audience and observing the person through the body—concepts related to art. "Contact Improvisation is the beauty of natural movement combined with full communication" (Curt Siddall in *Contact Quarterly* 3[Fall 1977]:3).

Thus, the body in contact improvisation ideally becomes the repository of the responsiveness and personality of the person. Properties often associated with mind in American culture—intelligence, judgement, communication—and with the emotions—tenderness, expression, spontaneity—are attributed to the body, thereby blurring commonly accepted categorizations of aspects of a person.

In some sense, the body and movement itself in contact improvisation are also synonymous with nature, because they follow natural laws of gravity, momentum, inertia, and so on. Feeling (physically) those forces, becoming swept away by disorientation (Nancy Stark Smith's phrases), represents a reality to the contact improviser which takes precedence over movement based on ideas (mind) separate from body, or feeling (emotion) separate from body. It is interesting that oneness with nature connects with both calm peacefulness and wild disorientation. The shared attribute of both is that mind and culture are receding and allowing body and nature to take over, bringing out the best aspects of the person.

The particular identification of dance with nature in contact improvisation confirms one part of the American modern dance tradition and repudiates another part of that tradition. All modern dancers have claimed some natural basis to their art, particularly in contrast with the ballet, which modern dancers have generally characterized as being relatively more artificial, unreal, and unnatural.[2] Yet modern dancers have also claimed a variety of sources other than natural law for their dancing —imaginative, dramatic, or intellectual conceptions which shaped and formed the natural impulses of movement and were thereby separated from the body. The body in these traditional forms often became conceptualized as an instrument of the art and of the creative mind rather than, as in contact improvisation, an intelligent practitioner of the art.

In sum, the image of the responsive body, which is not a mere reflex action but a mode of being in which the person is most in accord with

2. Early modern dancers were specifically interested in nature as a source for movement, for example, Isadora Duncan was inspired by dancing on the beach as a child, Mary Wigman drew images from natural forms, Doris Humphrey created studies of nature. For American modern dancers, this propensity has two formative historical roots in nineteenth-century America: an attachment in the American literary tradition to the pastoral ideal of the American frontier as a defense against industrialization and social change (see Marx 1964); and the search, on a popular level, for a redemptive, natural practice of physical fitness and health (see Green 1986 for an account of nineteenth-century health reform movements, and Kendall 1979, Ruyter 1979, and Shelton 1981 for discussions of the relationships between physical culture and modern dance).

natural law, constitutes a central symbol of contact improvisation. The concept of the responsive body is not a simple description of how the body is to be used in the dance form; it stands for an entire fabric of meanings. Ideally, the responsive body represents honesty, reality, spirituality, and the suppression of selfish, egotistical striving. At the same time, since the responsive body *is* the person, allowing the responsive body to act is felt to reveal the individual in a profound way.

Realizing the Responsive Body

Steve Paxton's original interests in examining movement outside of a traditional dance technique and in exploring delimited areas of movement found a perfect realization in the technical requirements of the contact improvisation form. He emphasized the physical possibilities of two bodies interacting improvisationally for a number of reasons. One reason was utilitarian: it was dangerous not to focus on the physical.

Paxton also recognized that an emphasis on physical experience would narrow the scope of the improvisation and keep it from dissipating into something vague or confusing. Consequently, the "contact," the possibilities of two bodies interacting in a particular way, became paramount. Paxton explained:

> Contact [improvisation] seemed to me to have the possibility of grounding us enough that we could talk about what the improvisation was . . . because we weren't skipping to emotional material and then on to something like group ritual material and then on to domestic references with props, like the Grand Union did. You were just laying dermis to dermis and moving around, trying to understand just that limited area.

By focusing on the physical body, Paxton anticipated questions about the role of self-expression in improvisation. Contact improvisers, however, have frequently debated the issue of what kind of self emerges from their activity. During the '70s, the differences which developed between the styles of the East and West coasts centered on this issue. Both the East and West Coast approaches to performance shared a sense that the emotions are connected to the body and that individuals are being revealed through movement. At issue seemed to be whether one focused the investigation on the body and "pure" movement (East Coast style) or whether one developed the comic or dramatic implications of movement as they emerged (West Coast style).[3]

Alan Ptashek, who lived in the San Francisco Bay Area but who had studied with East Coast dancers, contrasted the West Coast style of Mangrove with the East Coast style of the ReUnion group:

> The dancers in Mangrove were beautiful movers. There was some-thing, at their worst, that was campy and slapstick . . . but I don't think they intended that—that was not their overlying aesthetic. They wanted to infuse something lighter, more comical into the dancing . . . to get children at a contact performance laughing and seeing that grown men could be playful and crazy like kids . . . that was wonderful.
>
> Sometimes in the ReUnion performances, although they were magical in their way, sometimes the seriousness, the unanimated affect, the downward gaze . . . created a texture and density . . . that was limited, that did not give them access to other human conditions as performers. Mangrove wanted to open up the other end of things. . . .

John LeFan of Mangrove explained that the work of his company always grew from "the physical dance. At least for the first two or three years, *everything* Mangrove did began with contact and the dances and ideas came out of that." The members of Mangrove, many with backgrounds in theater, perceived the drama inherent in the physical relationships of the dancing and sought to extend that drama. LeFan suggested that those contact improvisers who thought that they could separate the body from the mind and do a "purely physical" dance were deluding themselves. Although he never thought Paxton believed this (citing highly theatrical dances which Paxton had made), LeFan felt that others deliberately tried to suppress emotion which might spring from the dancing.

The panel discussion at the St. Mark's conference in 1983 debated this topic, with Steve Paxton criticizing the "moodless dancing" he

3. Participants tended to characterize the East Coast style (which was not geographi-cally confined to the East Coast but which reached into places like Vancouver, where the East Coast teachers were influential) as pure contact improvisation. They tended to define the West Coast style, which also was not geographically confined, as more theatrical or dramatic.

thought was engendered by too simplistic a notion of the physical. At the same time, Paxton defended his original approach of beginning with body action:

> When you're beginning to learn about the unicorn [the third force generated by the interaction of two dancers—the "it"], if the only way you can communicate with somebody is to stop and chat, or if something funny happens, to stop and laugh, you basically get away from what you're there to study, and you're back into the verbal world. I feel like you're working through the wrong set of senses to understand what the work might reveal. . . . But at this point [1983], the only duets that I'm truly interested in or really engaged in are those that have all these things in strong measure that in fact I tended to push away initially (and still do for beginning students)—things like socializing, laughter, talking, eye contact, hand manipulation in contact. . . .

As one of the experimental dancers of the '6os, Paxton tried to shed the concept of a psychological domination of the body by the inner soul expressing itself through movement. Along with others, he posited the body as a sign in itself, replacing the image of the body dominated by an expressive inner self with the responsive body—mindful, feeling-filled, and physical. Ironically, over time this image coincided with obsessions in the larger culture with the body as an object of display and as a functional instrument for fulfilling tasks, even aesthetic tasks. Paxton's comments quoted above indicate the power of this American cultural image to co-opt the experimental "pure" movement of '6os choreographers. Their focus on the physical in dancing had been largely assimilated into the post-'6os emphasis on aerobics, fitness, sports, youth, and physical beauty.

Furthermore, the movement elements accepted from '6os dance into the canon of contemporary dance are precisely those elements—athleticism, endurance, unusual physical feats—which match popular mass cultural images. The complex countercultural notion of the body proposed by contact improvisation was (and is) difficult to maintain against the images of the body as beautiful object and virtuoso instrument.[4] Paxton's

4. Dance historian Susan Manning relates a telling anecdote about cultural difference. At a dinner party in New York for German modern dancer Susannah Linke, one of the American guests complimented Linke on her "fantastic, muscular body." Linke replied that, on her American tour (1985), all anybody wanted to talk about was her body and what

renewed interest in "laughter, talking, and eye contact" as they emerge from concentration on the physical body, represents an attempt to recapture the original vision of the practice in a changing artistic and cultural context.

Improvisation

The ramifications of the responsive body are extended by the fact that the body is not independent in contact improvisation. The spatial disorientation unique to the dance form derives from the fact that the center of weight in the body lies somewhere between two (or more) bodies and is constantly shifting. In one respect, body boundary becomes very clear, because one is so aware of touch and weight on the body surfaces; simultaneously, the body's boundaries are also experienced as being very flexible, because one's own sense of weight often merges with the weight of another and changes rapidly as body positions change.

On a technical level, the presence of another body as a lever or surface allows a dancer to do movements which are impossible to execute alone. The spatial dynamics of two bodies moving together produce part of the athleticism of the form, enabling certain kinds of lifts and falls that can be very spectacular to do and to watch. On the level of experience, this physical union of two dancers provides another key to part of the meaning of contact improvisation in American culture.

In contact improvisation, each person is conceived of as an individual yet cannot do the dance unless it is shared with another. Contact improvisation defines the self as the responsive body and also as the responsive body listening to another responsive body, the two together spontaneously creating a third force that directs the dance. The boundaries of the individual are crossed by "seeing through the body" and "listening through the skin," allowing the dance to unfold. In order to understand this aspect of how contact improvisation creates a way of dancing, the movement must be seen within the context of improvisation, the process through which the dance is generated.

At the level of cultural values, improvisation proposes dance-making as a collective action, in which directorial and creative authority resides with the group as a whole. At the same time, improvisation is seen to unify the roles of choreographer and dancer in each person, allowing

she looked like. "The Germans never talk about my appearance," she said. "They make up stories about what they think my dances mean."

the individual to make decisions about the dance and to observe herself or himself in action. "Improvisation," Steve Paxton has said, "gives you a chance to glance at yourself sideways as you move through time and space and to learn about your own behavior."

The collaborative element of improvisation can be seen to represent a joining of the values of individualism and egalitarianism, for the realization of the individual is placed within the context of cooperation and group activity rather than in the context of competition and personal achievement. For example, improviser David Appel recalled a turning point in his dance training when he was taking a class in aikido, in which "everyone helped everybody else to learn," and a class in modern dance technique in a professional New York studio, in which "everyone competed for the teacher's attention and approval." The differences between the two ways of working became clear to him, and he knew he wanted to find a way to dance in an atmosphere like that of the aikido class. He left New York to study with Steve Paxton in New England shortly thereafter. Improvisation in this instance became associated with the possibility of individual action within and through a cooperative, group setting.

Many observers of American life have commented on the centrality of concepts of individualism. In *Habits of the Heart: Individualism and Commitment in American Life* (Bellah et al. 1985), a comprehensive commentary on American cultural values, the authors point to four major traditions of individualism (and community) in America. The biblical tradition, impetus for the first utopian American settlements, envisions the formation of an ethical community in which freedom and justice are thought to be realized within a common code. The republican tradition, foundation of the American nation, posits active citizen participation as the basis on which individual freedom is realized. Utilitarian individualism proposes individual self-improvement (material and otherwise) as the means by which social good will emerge. And expressive individualism, the basis for self-immersion in experience (and a central ideal of American modernism in art), sees that "the ultimate use of America's independence was to cultivate and express the self and explore its vast social and cosmic identities" (35). The authors lament the dominance of utilitarian individualism, which they argue has overtaken American culture in the twentieth century. They point to a serious decline of biblical and republican ideals and to the separation of expressive notions of individualism from meaningful practices of collective life.

Contact improvisation, understood both as a social movement and an aesthetic tradition, speaks directly to these forms of American individualism while attempting to overcome the utilitarian emphasis Bellah and his colleagues decry. Improvisational dancers share the dance with one another for aesthetic reasons, because they think the outcome is something exciting and fascinating to watch and experience. Often, they also share the dance for ethical reasons, because they believe they can model certain moral and social aspects of their lives on this noncompetitive, collaborative form of dancing.

In addition to the dynamic of individual and collective action in improvisation, the concept of spontaneity is central, both aesthetically and ideologically. Improvisational dancers believe that they are making art while being spontaneous, a contrast to the worked-out, predetermined nature of traditional modern dance. Spontaneity signifies that the dancing is "real," "playful," and "natural," joining the making of art to everyday action. Dancer/choreographer Simone Forti articulated this aspect of contact improvisation when she first watched people practicing the form; "This is dance as art-sport," she observed.

On a symbolic level, improvisation in American dance is seen by its proponents as the unification of the opposites of individual and group activity. Theoretically, this unification occurs through the collaborative and egalitarian nature of making dances in which the individual experiences self-awareness and self-discovery. Improvisation also symbolically unites the opposites of nature and culture through both the emphasis on spontaneity (natural) and on the creation of dance art (cultural) and the emphasis on the joining of behavior (natural) with presentation (cultural).[5] Furthermore, for contact improvisers, the unification of nature and culture is very particular, because they conceive of the body as responsive to natural laws. "Drop a book, consciously or not, and it will fall"; contact improvisation is seen to demonstrate spontaneously and collectively the artful elements which characterize the behavior of the responsive body.

As with conceptions of nature and the body, ideas about improvisation differ among improvisational dancers, dancers in general, and different kinds of audiences.[6] Some dancers and dance viewers reject improvisation in performance, because, they argue, the dance needs to

5. This structural analysis of opposites contained within improvisational dance derives from Lévi-Strauss's proposal (1975) that human beings mediate the contradiction of their natural and cultural constitution through the union of opposites in symbolic life.

6. Improvisation changes historically as well. The history of improvisation in American dance has yet to be written; for a brief, summary account, see Matheson, forthcoming in 1991.

be worked out beforehand in order to qualify as art. Some also believe that improvisation is basically a participatory process, unpolished and indeterminate, and therefore not suited to being watched. For those who do advocate some kind of performance improvisation, disagreement exists about what kind of improvisation it should be. Some people relish seeing "someone out there on a limb," breaking out of known limits and displaying personal, impulsive risk-taking. Others reject performances which are "just exploring, going nowhere," and look for improvisations which focus on choreographic or conceptual ideas or which exert clear control over the shaping of material.

In fact, the polarities which emerge in doing and watching improvisation attest to the tension between elements united symbolically. Two major, often conflicting, polarities are evident, one aligned with the modern dance tradition in its emphasis on composition and intentional structuring, the other placed outside the boundaries of traditional art, with emphasis on behavior and personal impulse. The latter polarity is generally more widespread (and more commonly emphasized among contact improvisers); improvisation in American dance is most often expected to be concerned primarily with risky physical and psychological encounters and not with choreographic interactions.[7] This popular identification of improvisation with idiosyncratic behavior and personal impulse indicates the continuing strength of specific convictions popular in the '60s (and, periodically, throughout American history) that freedom and independence occur outside of structures. Conversely, it also attests to the persistence of the modern dance tradition of expressive individualism, which in practice tends to become unmoored from collective endeavor.

The tensions within improvisational dance articulate American cultural categories and associations, allowing for a particular kind of variation or interpretation within the dance form. These tensions or oppositions are not inherent, however, in all improvisational art forms. For instance, one would not find them in classical Indian dance and music or in West African dance and music, in which purposive action and spontaneity are not dichotomized or seen as opposites, and composition and improvisation are not counterposed.[8] They are also absent to a degree

7. American critical writing about dance prominently exhibits this point of view; dance criticism almost automatically assumes that improvisation is impulsive risk-taking as opposed to choreographic method.

8. See, for example, Holroyde 1972 and Vatsyayan 1968 for discussions of Indian dance and music, and Nketia 1974, Thompson 1963, and Chernoff 1983, for discussions of West African dance and music.

from American jazz music and tap dancing, both part of an African-American art tradition which tends not to conceive of expressiveness as being counter to control.

These dichotomies and implicit associations—culture/nature, art/behavior, choreography/process, structure/spontaneity, thought/feeling, control/intuition, mind/body, and, of course, male/female—have powerful effects on American dance. In contact improvisation, a temporary synthesis of some of these oppositions has been made possible. The concept of the responsive body, which when realized is both artful and natural, and the process of improvisation, which uses spontaneous action in the making of dance, have contributed to a joining of art and behavior. Furthermore, the absence of gendered attributes from the central symbols of contact improvisation has enabled a blurring of male/female distinctions. Given these values in conjunction with the formal structure and practice of the dancing, it is not surprising that many people have felt that contact improvisation offers the opportunity for a unique dance experience.

8
Community, Values, and Authority

In the early years of contact improvisation, the practice and development of the form occurred in scattered locations, on an ad hoc basis. A small group of dancers worked with some particular movement ideas, teaching each other and close friends and living companions as the situation arose, showing it to others when they had the opportunity. When the original group dispersed, people began gradually to organize classes and to train dancers who were to be the next generation of teachers and performers.

During this period of time, collective and communal living situations were somewhat common among many middle-class young adults. For the rehearsals for the first performance of contact improvisation at the John Weber Gallery in 1972, everyone lived and worked in the same loft. Nancy Stark Smith's first contact improvisation classes in California included the people from the Stinson Beach commune in which she was living. The early touring groups traveled, ate, and lived together as friends, "like a family" (the phrase used by several people). The clear divisions which often exist in a performance dance form like ballet—for example, distinctions between the significance of the dance studio and the rest of the world, or between the person in the role of a dancer and the person in other social roles—were not clearly delineated.[1] Dance and life overlapped and mingled for many participants in contact improvisation.

1. Toni Bentley (1982) describes her life with the New York City Ballet as one that felt both very special and totally isolated from the outside world.

Spontaneity and Decision-making

People who were involved with contact improvisation in the initial period recalled little discussion or planning about what was to happen in the future. Performances were frequently arranged at the last minute, and some of the dancers might have been meeting each other for the first time in a performance setting (possibly in any setting). The participants found it acceptable that the abilities of performers varied. The feeling conveyed when contact improvisers talked about the events of 1972–75 was that "they just happened"—opportunities arose, and everyone was willing to respond.

This description of social spontaneity corresponds directly to contact improvisers' conceptualizations of the dance form. In both the social and artistic realms, contact improvisers cultivated an atmosphere of spontaneity and characterized whatever decisions were consciously and overtly made as being necessary responses to practical matters. Concerts were "pulled together at the last minute"; "we never knew what we were going to do next"; "if something had to be organized, someone would do it—if not, it wouldn't happen."

Spontaneity, both organizational and artistic, thus came to represent the natural mode of decision-making, unfettered by manipulative thought; belief in spontaneity also seemed to generate a sense of egalitarianism, because nobody appeared to be imposing his or her will on anyone else—if everything just happens, who can be held responsible? When decisions about organization appear to be made only when necessary, practicality or utility in social organization becomes a parallel to the laws of gravity in dancing. Anyone who makes decisions "out of necessity" must simply take action and is therefore not imposing an ideology on everyone else.[2]

A crucial moment in the organization of the contact improvisation movement developed, as described in chapter 3, when the numbers of people practicing the dance form were increasing and moving to new locations and when questions were being raised about the safety of contact improvisation classes. This increase in numbers of participants and

2. What this point of view overlooks is the ideological content of any action, taken for whatever ostensible reason; different cultures have differing conceptions of what is practical and necessary. Utility is also, as Marshall Sahlins (1976) has argued, a central ideology of American culture.

their geographic dispersal caused some of the most active contact improvisers to feel proprietary towards the dance form and to want some kind of centralization. Contact improvisation was changing from an artistic experiment with dance to a social movement. Consequently, differentiating contact improvisation from other forms of dance took on more importance as a means of saying what contact improvisation was and of clarifying its uniqueness and social identity. Some definition of the dance form was also needed in order both to recruit new dancers and to keep the movement from fragmenting.

Concerns about self-definition, coherence, and safety were augmented by fears on the part of certain people over increasing competition among teachers. By 1975, dancers were beginning to make money from teaching contact improvisation. According to Alan Ptashek, those making part of their living from the teaching were reluctant to add new teachers, in part because they feared the new teachers were insufficiently prepared, but also because new teachers might mean less business. Conflict developed in San Francisco, for example, over a newer contact improviser beginning to teach in the Bay Area—conflict which never prevented the new teacher from offering classes but which generated a certain amount of discord.

As noted earlier, in 1975 the "core" contact improvisers proposed that they form a company, certify new teachers, collect a percentage of individual earnings, and work through a manager. The fact that a group of people with an ideology of spontaneity would have considered such an elaborate proposal for institutionalization appears incongruous. Yet it seems that the largely unstated nature of the ideology of contact improvisation in the early years, combined with the informality of their organization, allowed the group to more or less stumble into the proposed arrangement. No less significant was the overwhelming presence of similar institutions in the professional dance world. The organization of the dance world existed as a model for how to cope with the difficulties of self-definition and economic competition, and such institutionalization was proposed as an immediate solution to problems and as a kind of natural evolution of a dance form.

However, after people outlined the proposal, the ideological contradictions were simply too overt for the contact improvisers to accept them; perhaps more important, no one wanted to take on so much organizational responsibility. Also, Paxton opposed the idea, fearing that excessive regulation would destroy the flexibility of the movement and formally place him in a leadership role, about which he was ambivalent. Subsequently, the original group decided not to enforce rules to certify teachers or to label members of the group officially but, instead, to start the *Contact Newsletter* as a means for education and discussion about the dance form. Participants in contact improvisation in the '70s saw this decision as a watershed in the history of contact improvisation. It signaled collective possession of the dance form by anyone who wanted to practice it while it simultaneously conferred great moral authority on the leaders who had rejected direct control, particularly Steve Paxton as the initiator of the form and as the primary opponent of incorporation.

This act by Paxton contrasted with other modern dance choreographers' overt attempts to protect and control their material and has been a key factor in the nature of Paxton's leadership. He has been able to exert significant influence on the contact improvisation movement, without appearing to seek that role and even while appearing to reject it. Other contact improvisers have given him recognition because of this tacit moral stance. At the same time, the absence in contact improvisation of a single figure who controls the dance technique has also enabled participants to identify as much with a way of dancing and living as with a particular person. This characteristic appears unusual in the history of modern dance, in which individual choreographers always combined their explorations of new forms with directing and shaping their own visions using a company of dancers, and in which the dancers felt the work belonged to the choreographer.

According to several personal accounts, the decision not to certify and incorporate evolved easily, with people feeling from the beginning that it would turn out that way, no matter what steps might be taken, because the work could *not* be formally organized. Nancy Stark Smith offered her view of the event:

> At that point, I realized how unorganizable this work is. It's based on the premise of individuals, even though it has a lot to do with unity, harmony, and all of that. It has everything to do with freedom and not with institutions. So every attempt to codify it, to organize it, to regulate it, has been unsuccessful. That doesn't mean that various contact companies weren't able to organize themselves; certainly, that's their own free will to do that. But it was never said what the guidelines were that would tell you whether what you were doing was contact improvisation or not. It

was more unspoken. Over time you would know, and you would
know for yourself, not because somebody wrote it somewhere.

The underlying sentiments in Smith's remarks mirror religious and
political beliefs deep in the American Protestant and Populist traditions.
Protestantism emphasizes the immediate connection of each individual
to God in contrast with Catholicism's good works which earn one a place
in the Church. Smith's comments translate the American allegiance to
individualism and the religious rights of the individual over institutions
into an artistic independence and a right to be part of a collective dance
form without being directly imposed upon. Democracy and freedom are
respected as artistic rights embodied in contact improvisation, and even
free enterprise is accepted on the grounds that, after all, everyone may
do as he or she wishes. At the same time, the nature of the improvisational process maintains equality. "Improvisation allows dancers to keep
their motive, rather than turning it over to a choreographer," Paxton has
suggested. "Or you could say, the motive is handed over to an equal, not
a master. It's more like a conversation."

The dance form itself thus posed social values seen to be inherent
in its very structure. Said Ellen Elias, "It wasn't that people who did contact were any nicer than anybody else . . . it's just that the structure of
contact supported people being decent, supported people being gentle,
caring, loving." Contact improvisation provided a metaphorical framework for thinking about social life. "Contact presented an approach to
harmonious interaction, providing a model for people communicating
and collaborating," suggested Gurney Bolster. "It set up a framework for
leaders and followers to exchange roles." Charles Campbell of Mangrove
(the all-men's performance collective, San Francisco) wrote:

> It's clear to me that we are exploring new personal/political/
> artistic ground for ourselves, as men gently (and aggressively) sup-
> porting each other in a non-hierarchical collective improvisational
> process, and sharing that process in performance, from a position
> of vulnerability and humor and fear, too. . . . it's all about us as
> people and as men finding the "people things" which happen in
> our process of coming into contact. (1980:6)

Campbell's comments counterpose the creative possibilities he sees offered to men by contact improvisation with the limitations of the roles he
believes men can play in hierarchical, individualistic, more traditionally

structured circumstances. Campbell's remarks indicate that the redefinition of gender roles by the use of the body and movement in contact improvisation was simultaneously extended to signify a challenge to other aspects of gender roles in American culture, particularly the constraints on men to be strong and invulnerable. Again, participants experienced the dancing itself as social and political.

The articulation of contact improvisation's meaning in social terms revealed several kinds of interpretations. In part, this discussion elaborated on the significances of the movement qualities inherited from their '60s environment. In part, it also served to address the conflicts engendered by the attempt, in the context of American culture, to be individuals and yet not compete, to express disagreements and yet not impose oneself on another person, and to be organized without having an "organization." Finally, ideological definition served as a means of distinguishing contact improvisation as a dance form and as a social movement from other kinds of dance.

Participation and Performance:
Contact Improvisation as a "Folk Art"

One of the early ways in which contact improvisers defined themselves was to label their dance a folk art. Although the label was very loosely and casually applied, considering the applicability of the term raises interesting questions. Anthropologists and folklorists have generally characterized "folk art" as an art which is locally based, founded on a communal tradition, and often overtly functional, particularly in the plastic arts (Glassie 1970; Real 1977). Like other dances called folk forms, contact improvisation was locally based around communities; however, instead of organizing around traditional communities defined by rural location or ethnic origin, contact improvisation communities consisted of mostly young, middle-class whites located in cities and towns across the country with little or no recognized ethnic identity. The center of contact improvisation has never been New York City, the base of the professional American dance world; contact improvisation was founded on a countercultural communal tradition which evolved in each location.

One could even take the analogy further: although fulfilling no utilitarian function, contact improvisation had an aesthetic and a social structure of utility—the primary object of the dance has been to explore the

"physics" of two bodies moving, and if someone wanted to do it, she or
he had to teach it to other people in order to have partners. Thus, like
a folk dance, it attracted the participation of people who would never
have considered taking an "art" dance class in ballet or modern dance
and who wanted a social experience as part of their dancing.

In addition to being what could be called a folk dance, contact improvisation has also been a performance form. Thus people can interpret
it in different ways, believing that they are communicating and expressing themselves in activity that is meaningful to watch (a function usually
attributed to art in America), and/or feeling that they are interacting with
other people (a function usually attributed to social dance in America).
In either case, the activity has had a practical, utilitarian cast; the dance
"arose" because physical law elicited the movement, its meaning a result
of its natural effect, and the social organization of the dancers arose out
of simple necessity.

The "folk" characteristics of contact improvisation coexisted with its
performance characteristics for a period of at least five years, from its
inception in 1972 until the late '70s. Lisa Nelson recalled:

> Contact improvisation really was a folk dance form in the early
> '70s—the whole concept of jams and getting together with people.
> It was a complete folk form–social form at first and the show-
> ings were just that—going to show more people so you could get
> together with them to dance. I would always drop in on jams,
> wherever I was. . . . I'd meet new people and dance and walk out
> feeling like something really had happened.

The social or folk attributes of contact improvisation distinguished
it from other kinds of modern dance, including improvisational modern dance, although there were a number of individual dance companies
scattered throughout the country which worked on a collective or collaborative basis throughout the '70s and '80s. In fact, however, the folklike
nature of contact improvisation has constituted an exception to virtually
all American art dance, both modern and ballet.[3]

For a part of its history, contact improvisation on a small scale resembled dance forms from other cultures of the world, cultures in which

---

3. Another exception, tap dance, has historically relied on informal teaching and
social gatherings as ways to learn the dancing, exchange ideas, and engage in friendly
competition.

people conceive of dance as part of their social identity. For example, in many West African societies, virtually everyone participates in dance to some degree, because it constitutes an acknowledged and important part of numerous social occasions. Although these people recognize skilled dancers and enjoy seeing them perform, their performances often take place in the context of what Americans would consider social or folk dancing. Virtuoso performance and recognition of social values and occasions are not necessarily separated, nor are participation and performance dance always two different categories.[4]

In contrast, twentieth-century American art dance, by its definition as an art form, has been separated from the social life of most people and has been defined as a professional (work) activity for the performers and a recreational or leisure activity for the audience. Contact improvisation, if only for a short period of time or in particular places, constituted a dance form which allowed for a range of participation outside of the structure of a dance class or dance company, a participation which included both social dancing and a sense of performing or of showing dance to others. As an exception, contact improvisation points to the rule that dance in American culture is highly categorized and differentiated. The difficulty which contact improvisers eventually experienced in maintaining a unity between the different aspects of contact improvisation also attests to the fact that it is a rare occurrence when these categories can be transcended.

Steve Paxton as a Charismatic Authority

Social movements proposing alternatives to mainstream values and patterns of behavior with the kind of cohesiveness that contact improvisation exhibited often originate in and rely on the charisma of a single leader. Max Weber used the term "charisma" to describe the leadership of a wide range of religious, political, and artistic movements inspired by people who have been considered "holders of specific gifts of the body and spirit. . . . In contrast to any kind of bureaucratic organization of offices, the charismatic structure knows nothing of a form or of an ordered procedure of appointment or dismissal. . . . Charisma knows only inner determination and inner restraint" (1967:245–46). Weber also suggested

4. John Chernoff (1983) provides a detailed account of the complex nature of West African music and dance and their realization of both aesthetic and social meanings.

that "charisma, and this is decisive, always rejects as undignified any pecuniary gain that is methodical and rational" (247).

In significant ways, Steve Paxton's leadership of contact improvisation was charismatic. Throughout the early years of contact improvisation, Steve Paxton stood as a key figure to whom people looked for leadership. The absence of rationalization and bureaucracy in the social organization of contact improvisation and the simultaneous strength of Paxton's influence mark the development of the dance form.

When contact improvisation began, the group of people practicing it had a communal, egalitarian structure except for the fact that Steve Paxton was looked to as the teacher and the informal director. The social organization of the dancers involved with contact improvisation was much looser and more democratic than that of a traditional dance company, because no one was in direct control of what other dancers did. As younger dancers began teaching, and even performing on their own, they began to participate, with Paxton, in the informal leadership of their emerging community.

Yet Paxton's opinions undoubtedly held the greatest influence within the group, particularly in the early years, even though he made a conscious effort to pull back from the role of a choreographer leading a dance company. "When I organize things, I become a compulsive organizer," he explained. "That means I hardly ever organize anything, because it's such a hassle. . . . A company just seemed an enormous barrier to getting any work done, and I didn't want that dictatorship which was given a director by a company." At the same time, Paxton played a major role through his teaching, performing, and writing, and he frequently expressed his opinions about the direction of that development in an attempt to influence others' understanding of it. His prominence meant that his invitations to perform carried great weight; for example, Paxton's choice of whom to invite and not invite to Rome in 1973 generated several lasting resentments.

Over the years, Steve Paxton has influenced more dancers than most people who have established dance companies. He has done so because of his specific talents and interests in movement, which coincided with a particular historical moment, a moment which allowed him to be perceived as a holder of "specific gifts of the body and spirit" by a large group of people. Paxton's orientation toward exploring extremes of movement, toward improvisation, and toward nonhierarchical organizations coincided with a social ambiance favoring experimentation, spontaneity, and egalitarianism.

Paxton's personal style, variously described by contact improvisers as intense, disciplined, ascetic, inspiring, forbidding, and brilliant, made him ideally qualified to lead a movement which rejected formal leadership. Paxton is seen to have earned respect and admiration by his actions, none of which involved overtly taking power. Ironically, the action of rejecting power served in many instances to heighten Paxton's informal power and influence; people became even more fascinated by and admiring of him as he alternately took and shunned the spotlight.

Paxton was caught in a state of paradox, of being a leader because he did not overtly lead. Nancy Stark Smith has said that he held "a leadership position in a vacuum"; writer Deborah Jowitt has aptly described Paxton's demeanor while teaching class as "a curious blend of the noncommittal and the messianic" (1977). Paxton was not always happy with the situation (nor were all of his colleagues), because he had committed himself ideologically to egalitarian methods of generating dancing. In a 1981 interview, when Paxton was asked about a possible new direction for contact improvisation stemming from an idea he had just presented, he replied:

> "I don't know, because there's this whole thing of leadership in improvisational situations . . . when you are trained to do contact, you have a teacher and you follow instructions and this is antithetical to an improvisational way; it creates a dependency, it's a hierarchical situation, and I think that that has to be obliterated at some point. The students have to be made aware of it so that they take over their own responsibility for the training. So if I go ahead now at this point, create new steps in the technique, I'm reinforcing a hierarchy that implicitly exists in the situation. I will remain a leader-figure, and I'm not sure that is healthy. . . . What I would like is that other people would just take off, and take over their own responsibility and do their own investigations, based on the possibilities this form has presented. In other words, use the form as a model." (Transcribed in Paxton 1981–82:18)

I would argue that Paxton's ambivalent leadership was a major force which held the movement together in the '70s, that the elements of paradox and even inconsistency were part of his strength, one of his particular gifts of body and spirit. His ambivalence allowed for flexibility: for speaking out when necessary and pulling back when possible, so that he asserted clarity of vision and direction at the same time that he made allowances for others to provide leadership. Paxton's embodiment of charismatic authority was such that it ideally suited the leadership of this particular antitraditional, antirational, anti-authoritarian movement.

As the years have passed, Paxton has played less and less of a leadership role (teaching and performing less, as well), with local artists becoming prominent in the late '70s and with Nancy Stark Smith stepping into a national leadership role in the mid-'80s as the most active teacher and performer and as co-editor of the *Contact Quarterly*. Yet Paxton still carries considerable authority. As Smith noted to me, her own leadership role stems in part from her proximity to Paxton, with whom she has performed contact improvisation since its inception.

Contact Improvisation as a National Movement

Through the '70s, the national connections of the locally based contact improvisation communities gave contact improvisation a sense of being a movement, part of the wave of social movements which had swept America since the '60s. The sense of belonging to a larger entity helped make local contact improvisation groups cohesive and established a public face for contact improvisation.

These characteristics help to explain the rapid growth and spread of contact improvisation. However, not everyone interested in contact improvisation wanted to be a part of a movement, and some disliked the "cultlike" atmosphere that surrounded some contact improvisation groups. One dancer who had been active in the early years of the movement gradually stopped doing contact improvisation, because, although she found the dancing "so exciting" in the beginning, after a while it disturbed her to see "people performing contact who were imitating Steve's [Paxton] or Nancy's [Stark Smith] movement characteristics. They looked like little clones, and that seemed the direct opposite of what the dance form was supposed to be about." Lisa Nelson said that she never wanted to be called a contact improviser, that it bothered her to be labeled and to be associated with a large group of people she did not even know. Nancy Stark Smith suggested that people who learn contact improvisation often "pass through a phase" of believing it the only dance form worth doing, the most real and complete way to dance, displaying a kind of "contact chauvinism."

The suggestion that contact improvisation was a cult has also been made by dancers who did not participate in it. "Contact improvisers always seem to think that dance began with contact improvisation," one professional dancer complained. "They are just like ballet dancers," said another (a modern dancer); "they can't believe anyone else knows anything about movement that they don't know." At the 1980 American Dance Guild conference on improvisation (Dance as Art-Sport), a degree of subterranean grumbling occurred among some of the dancers who did not know contact improvisation, who felt that the presence of the contact improvisers dominated the conference and made others feel excluded. "Where I come from," reported one woman at the conference, "I'm considered too far out because I don't do ballet, and here, I feel like I'm uptight because I don't do contact improvisation."

If there was an atmosphere of exclusiveness within certain contact improvisation groups, as perceived by these dancers, its source lay in social ethos and organization. Contact improvisation, because it emphasized communality to a greater degree than other dance forms and because it overtly symbolized social values, often generated a passionate loyalty among participants. Although in virtually every American dance form, certain participants believe they are dancing in the best possible way and dismiss all other forms of dance,[5] people defending contact improvisation were for a time defending not just a way to dance but also an entire group with whom they shared their lives and their values. The sensibility of a "folk" form and the presence of charismatic authority heightened this self-definition.

The atmosphere of exclusiveness surrounding some contact improvisation groups, particularly in the late '70s, thus resulted from the distinctive identity which has made contact improvisation visibly different from any other kind of dance organizationally. The organization of most dance forms is simultaneously more contained and more fragmented than contact improvisation has been; most dance forms are organized solely within dance classes and individual performing companies led by single directors/choreographers. Contact improvisation has been orga-

---

5. This factionalism has pervaded American modern dance. Although many dancers study more than one modern dance technique, many others take classes only from a single school or teacher and claim unique superiority for their school.

nized not only in classes and performing groups with local leaders, but also in jams and dances, in ad hoc touring, in a national social network, through periodic national meetings, and through a national publication. Perhaps more important, the structure of contact improvisation has theoretically enabled *all* participants to feel that they could dance independently of a choreographer or director. Although the contact improvisation movement was fairly small, between a thousand and two thousand people nationally, the dance world clearly noticed its presence because it was so unified, and people who were not a part of it could have easily perceived themselves as "outsiders," just as participants could have felt themselves to be "insiders."

The national structure of contact improvisation has actually allowed for participation on many different levels by people with different attitudes. Some dancers have been oriented towards performance and only loosely connected to the social practice of the form. Said Danny Lepkoff, "I never really liked jams. There were too many people. I liked dancing when I felt my energy was visible in the space, and I was generally more interested in performance." Many other dancers have participated solely in classes and in social dance occasions, never becoming involved in performance.

A number of dancers dropped in and out of the movement, dancing or performing for a while, then doing other things, then coming back to jams again, and so on. At the 1983 conference at St. Mark's, Steve Paxton suggested that the flexibility of the contact improvisation community, its cultivation of "casual intimacy," has enabled it to last, because "very little is at stake" when people either join or drop out:

> It's almost like you're following your own mind—if you're slightly interested, or interested, or on up that scale, then it's easy to be in it. If you're not interested, very uninterested or bored, then you're not a part of it, probably, and that's about the scale of it. It only survives through actual interest; that's the energy that's maintaining it.

Contact improvisation began as a "folk" dance of largely unattached, mobile, young, middle-class people for whom a community of shared interests in the responsive body and egalitarian interaction was, at least for a while, a perfect vehicle for social life.

Hierarchy and Egalitarianism

The model for the social organization of contact improvisation existed in the organization of social movements in the '6os. According to Steve Paxton, working with the Judson Church group in the early '6os was his first experience in trying to create a dance situation which was "relatively nonhierarchical." In a 1977 interview, he explained:

> "You form a kind of hierarchy for practicality's sake, like the person with the best organizational skills may take over adminis- tration or stage management. But you don't have rigid social or class structure going down in a group. The kind of energy that I seem to enjoy most is one where I sense the potential from every- body who's around. Their integrity is intact and if needs be, one of them could take over part of the practical or organizational things." (Quoted in McDermott 1977:6)

Paxton's comments exemplify the ethos of practicality and the valuing of what might be called an egalitarian meritocracy. Some people have special skills which might be called upon, but no one holds permanent control as a result of his or her skills. Each person is an equal member who could take responsibility if necessary.

In a videotaped interview, made as a part of the Judson Project at Bennington College in 1983, Paxton acknowledged the inequality which arises within egalitarian systems. Nancy Stark Smith, conducting the interview, asked him if there was some kind of hierarchy when the mem- bers of the Judson Church group met collectively to decide which pieces to show in performance and in what order. Paxton replied:

> I'd say there were a lot of hierarchies going on. There was the offi- cial way we did business, which was Quaker method—agreement. There was [underlying that the question of] who was just a strong talker and discusser of issues, who made work that knocked every- body else out, who made work that was unpopular. . . . I wouldn't say there was *a* hierarchy, though. I'd say there were a lot of power things mixing in and out.

Anthropologist Louis Dumont has suggested that the ideals of liberty and equality derive from "the conception of man as an individual." Each individual can potentially do or become anything and must be treated as equal to any other. However, as soon as a group of people adopt a collective end, "their liberty is limited and their equality brought into question" (1966:11). Dumont's analysis continues an argument begun by Tocqueville about conflicts in American society, proposing that "to adopt a value is to introduce hierarchy." Because a certain consensus of values and a certain hierarchy of ideas, things, and people are "indispensable to social life," the ideal of equality is unattainable, even if people think it superior (20).

Dumont proposes that the concept of equality among individuals will inevitably be challenged by hierarchies arising from social roles and social action defined by the very concept of equality. He does not defend the use of power and control in hierarchy, but rather attempts to separate hierarchy from the automatic association it has with power and control in Western culture. Contact improvisation has embraced values of individualism, equality, and antihierarchical relationships. Yet if Dumont is right, one would expect contradictions to appear between these values and the differences which developed as a result of social roles and social action.

In addition, for those people who eventually became involved with contact improvisation on a professional basis, who taught and/or performed the dance as a means of living, a great deal was at stake in the organizational dynamics of the contact movement. The spate of local group organization which occurred from 1977 to 1979, as well as the increase in touring by individuals and by ad hoc groups, had the effect of promoting role distinctions within the movement. Differences between amateurs and professionals, between the less skilled and the very skilled, and between the social dancers and the performers developed rapidly as some dancers began to rely on contact performance as a professional identity expressed in paid appearances. Lisa Nelson, after talking about the "folk" nature of early contact improvisation, commented: "Eventually a lot of people became teachers and that started to change things . . . if you'd been performing, that kind of became a habit and you wanted to keep performing . . . after a while, it took you away from just being 'a folk' and spending time with 'the people.'"

Inevitably, the ideology of egalitarianism and spontaneity was challenged by the appearance of implicit hierarchy and overt planning. The demands of performing and operating within the professional dance world—promoting one's work, applying for grants, seeking students—involved these dancers in concerns somewhat different from those of the people who were participating in contact improvisation for social and recreational reasons.

Dancers were often differentiated from each other on a more informal basis. Some emerging differences were simply based on the level of skill individual participants brought to dance events: everyone began to know who the most able dancers were. Elizabeth Zimmer recalled her perceptions of the contact improvisation jams in Vancouver:

> There *was* a hierarchy. People tried to pretend there wasn't, but people who could really move got to dance with the people who could really move . . . like if I would ask Andrew Harwood to dance, we would dance for a while and then he'd say he wanted to stop and then he'd go on to dance with somebody who could really dance. So I'd consider it a good day if I got a couple of minutes with Peter [Ryan] and a couple of minutes with Andrew. So there were people you didn't want to dance with because they couldn't, other people you were reluctant to ask because they were so good, and depending on how you were feeling about yourself on any given day, you took certain kinds of risks.

Those who were very skilled or very involved in developing the dance form often found their interests diverging from the increasing numbers of new and relatively unskilled contact improvisers, as well as from those long-time improvisers who were primarily interested in dancing as social interaction. For example, in 1979, two large gatherings of contact improvisers took place. Current Exchange, a month-long meeting at the Western Front artists' cooperative in Vancouver, was organized by Steve Paxton for "serious students" of contact improvisation.[6] Those wishing to attend had to submit letters to Paxton describing their activities and interests, because Paxton did not want to teach or be in a position of responsibility for the group. The conference involved dancing (teaching, performing, jamming), discussion, writing, and video-making, a full-time endeavor for people with a strong involvement in the dance form. Country Jam, an event held that same year on Vancouver Island, was, according to Peter Ryan, "exactly the opposite of Current Exchange." Ryan, who attended and helped organize both events, laughingly de-

6. A smaller gathering had been organized the previous year by Paxton and Nancy Stark Smith; in 1979, Paxton and Lisa Nelson facilitated the conference.

scribed Country Jam as "dance for the proletariat . . . it was homespun, there was organic food and jamming every day." Participants ranged from beginning contact improvisers to those with extensive experience.

Ellen Elias, who attended Current Exchange, felt that it was "elitist" because of the requirement to write a letter, even though everyone who wrote was accepted. Among contact improvisers, she said, "there was a way of being elitist that was subtle . . . there was definitely a sense of in-group, out-group, but it was supposed to not be there." Like Zimmer, Elias noted the social convention of assumed equality which overlay the existence of differences in abilities and social roles.

What is particularly notable about the contact improvisation community during the late '70s is not that hierarchies and differences existed but that many participants were so conscious of them and disturbed by them. Although many contact improvisers actively promoted the idea that an experienced dancer should be able to dance with anyone and learn something from it, as the movement developed many questioned how true it was to this principle. At the 1980 American Dance Guild conference, a discussion, "Politics and Contact Improvisation," focused on the problem of "elitism" and the "exclusivist attitudes" of the "contact heavies" (Zientara 1980). People felt strongly that the egalitarian aspects of contact improvisation needed to be emphasized.

As the years passed, cultivating a spirit of trust and caring between partners has remained a central component of contact improvisation classes and jams, and has extended to the social ethos of communal organizations like Dance New England. On a social basis, egalitarian participation was not to be sacrificed to the special abilities of a few people. But this ethos has been very difficult to maintain, both within the context of performing and within the larger cultural and social circumstances of American life.

Coherence and Competition:
The American Dance Guild Conference

Despite its problems, the contact improvisation movement achieved a remarkable sense of community and flexibility throughout the '70s. The unities and conflicts among improvisational dancers as a larger entity provide an interesting comparison to the developments of the contact improvisation movement. The American Dance Guild conference in 1980, Improvisation: Dance as Art-Sport, offered a chance to make this comparison and to observe contact improvisation as a distinct social unit at a peak in its development.

There, a common sentiment heard about the conference, both in public statements and private conversations, was that it represented a community of people who share commitment to many of the same ideas and goals about dance. This sentiment echoes statements often made at other conferences and large gatherings of dancers such as awards ceremonies.

This community of dancers at large actually consists of a fragmented collection of dancers, located around individual dance companies, or small groups of associates organized around dance schools, dance departments in universities, performance spaces, or dance festivals. The groups within the community often compete. Even the experimental Judson Church dance group of the early '60s, which has assumed almost mythical historical proportions as an experiment in dance community, lasted two years as a loose association and stimulated personal jealousies and conflicts as well as cooperation and friendships.

Although many contemporary American dancers and choreographers know each other or know of each other, little basis for community activity exists outside of their mutual commitment to dance. The fact that dancers and choreographers must compete against each other at almost every level—for a teacher's or choreographer's attention, for teaching and performing jobs, for grant money, and for critical attention and favor —severely weakens this mutuality. Dancers complain vigorously in private about this situation, but their public comments seldom allude to it. Of necessity, as protection against a culture that generally sees dance as frivolous and irrelevant, dancers take a public stance of mutual understanding and support for the dance community.

At the American Dance Guild conference, the implicit social beliefs underlying the symbols of improvisational dance heightened ambivalences. People expressed pride in the idea that everyone can have access to improvisational dance and that the individual can realize herself or himself to a degree not allowed by traditional modern dance. The communal nature of group improvisation was seen to support an atmosphere of mutual trust. People expressed attitudes of tolerance and acceptance of differences, and commented on the atmosphere of cooperation and lack of overt competition at the conference.

Awareness of competition and hierarchies was generally submerged. On occasion, dancers spoke of art being turned into a commodity in

American society, and they talked about the competition and resentments within traditional modern dance groups, but for the most part,
no one wanted to recognize that improvisational dance might be subject
to the same conditions as any other kind of dance. In the panel discussion "Dance and Sport," Charles Moulton commented on the existence of
competition in both sport and improvisational dance, producing a burst
of nervous laughter.

The major exception at the conference to avoidance of mentioning
competition was the speech given by Anna Halprin, who was receiving
an award from the American Dance Guild for outstanding contribution
to the field of dance. Halprin, in a highly dramatic and intentionally hu-
morous speech, confessed her bitterness about the lack of recognition of
her work and at the fame of certain of her students, better known than
she. The performance context of Halprin's speech, the joking attitude of
it, and the contrasting condition of Halprin's receiving an award allowed
such a speech to be made without tension and embarrassment.

In general, organizers of the conference exerted strong efforts to
give everyone opportunity to teach and perform; the democratic premises of the conference led to the scheduling of numerous classes, panel
discussions, and spoken presentations by over sixty different people, an
enormous number for a dance conference. Yet groupings and hierarchies
existed, which some people resented.

The most highly recognized dancers not only received artistic prestige but also appeared to represent relative social and economic stability.
Although fourteen groups appeared in the two evening concert presentations, Free Lance Dance, the contact improvisation group with Steve
Paxton, Nancy Stark Smith, Lisa Nelson, Christie Svane, and Danny Lepkoff, presented its own concert, with no other group on the program,
as the final concert of the conference. Some noncontact improvisers
complained that the contact improvisers had taken over the conference
and were dominating everything; some contact improvisers expressed
resentment at "all those other people" outside of their particular community. Longtime Dance Guild members complained about the narrow-
mindedness of the younger dancers and about their ignorance of dance
history and their naive conviction that they were doing something totally
new. And some of the younger dancers expressed impatience at the con-
servative views of other participants.

The most well-defined social group, indeed the only close social community, at the Dance Guild conference was clearly that of contact impro-

visation. The larger culture of improvisational dance as a whole, and, to a degree, that of modern dance in general, seemed to bind people together only temporarily. Not only are most improvisational dancers generally isolated from one another in their daily work, but they must also compete with one another in order to pursue their art. Furthermore, because experience in American culture so often combines the values of individualism and self-expression with an ideology of free enterprise and competition, improvisational dancers find themselves in an extremely contradictory situation. Their belief in individuality can be made to fit the treatment of dance as a commodity, and, in order to survive as artists, improvisational dancers must, to a certain extent, participate in the dance market. Yet in order to pursue their other beliefs about improvisational dance—the central commitments to spontaneity and to collaboration—they feel the constraints of that market and need also to operate outside of it in some way in order to survive as artists.[7]

To the extent that contact improvisation became and remains a performance form, it, too, has been affected by these same constraints. By 1985, the contact improvisation movement was transformed so that it hardly constituted a movement any more; instead, it increasingly resembled either other forms of modern dance (if one looked at performing dancers) or social dance (if one looked at nonperforming contact improvisation dancers). Perhaps developments like these truly mark the end of the '60s.

7. Although the situation of improvisational dancers seems particularly problematic, similar kinds of conditions apply to many other kinds of American artists. Certainly the conflict between personal beliefs and social circumstances has been a frequent, often bitter experience throughout American modern dance history.

9
The Business of Performance

The particular interpretations of contact improvisation, like those of all cultural events, have varied depending on the situation and historical period. In time, the changes were profound enough to shift the major character of the dance form. It has changed from artistic experiment, to national movement, to a diverse practice of individual choreographers and dancers, localized social groups, and teachers. At first, participants were organized as small groups of devoted dancers, then a larger, more varied national organization with some cohesiveness of shared values and norms, and finally, an even larger number of practitioners engaged in very different activities. The history of contact improvisation draws the analyst's attention both to the trajectory of development in an art form and to the interaction of that art form with its surrounding social and economic contexts.

The early performances of contact improvisation were essentially demonstrations of the form, following the round robin format (see chapter 3). By 1976–77, some four years later, dancers began to feel that a demonstration of the form was not sufficient, and decisions had to be made about how to present the dancing. This perspective grew out of pressures both internal and external to the contact improvisation movement. Internally, the technique had developed to the point where dancers could display greater aesthetic and technical possibilities; they were no longer dealing with the purely investigative and experimental but were beginning to play with known elements of movement to find out what could be done with them. As a result, many dancers were anxious to define or explore related areas (such as using text or music, or structuring movement in ways outside the parameters of contact improvisation), and the original structure for presentation was no longer sufficient.

Externally, contact improvisation gained recognition at the same time as the social atmosphere supporting informal demonstration began to change. Showing the dance form in order to recruit new dancers and to expand audiences faded as a dominant motive. Dancers began to think more about the public impression of what they were doing and how they as individuals were doing it. They thus brought a certain consciousness of performance as a public validation of skill and artistry to what was formerly a demonstration of a new dance form.

Using the Dance Form as a Model for Action

These developments posed problems for a movement based upon strong opposition to hierarchy and authority. Who decides what to do and how performances are to be organized and funded when no one is supposed to dictate to anyone else? How is cohesion maintained as more and more people experiment with a dance form? Some participants debated these issues on a national level, in the pages of the *Contact Quarterly*, which proudly acknowledged the fact that different interpretations of the dance form were arising. Although some people expressed disapproval of certain developments or raised questions about their artistic quality, no one censored these developments. Perhaps the only person who would have had the authority to act as censor was Steve Paxton, and he did not do so. Instead, he exerted his influence less formally through his articles in the magazine and through his extensive personal contact with people and with audiences as he toured. Certainly, the entire traveling and touring network was crucial to maintaining coherence and creating clearer definitions of contact improvisation; those who performed frequently established a public image of the dancing.

In fact, the casual opinions of the most active teachers and dancers frequently exerted a powerful influence and an indirect means of control. For example, Lois Welk, a dancer in Binghamton, New York, choreographed a piece in 1977 called "6-5-4." The dance was structured around a twelve-measure phrase of choreographed movement, which repeated; with each repetition, contact improvisation replaced more and more of the original set phrase. Welk's experiment was to find out how to contain the contact improvisation within varying time frames and how to segue back and forth between set movement and contact improvisation. Welk reported later, "I heard through the grapevine that Nancy Stark Smith didn't like controlling the contact improvisation and felt that I was doing something impure with the pure style. I'm not sure what was said about it, but I got the vibes that the veterans didn't like it." The disapproval Welk sensed over her dance came "through the grapevine," but it disturbed her enough so that when she received an opportunity to perform her dance in a concert at Clark Center in New York City, she wrote to Steve Paxton about the piece, wanting "to clear it with him." Paxton replied with a postcard: "Sounds wonderful. Do whatever you want. Steve."

When I related this incident to Nancy Stark Smith in 1985, she was astonished because she did not remember hearing or saying anything about Welk's piece; all she knew about it was that she had printed a score for the dance in an issue of *Contact Quarterly* which had been set up to record "different ways people were using contact in performance." She added, "I'm sure that probably there was a force exerted by the so-called veterans that I was really not very aware of. . . . To be in a position of having whatever you say, even casually . . . get passed along and mean anything more than your personal opinion is an awkward position to be in." Whatever the actual facts of this particular story, it demonstrates the informal mechanisms of influence which surfaced as contact improvisation grew from an informal movement to a more established artistic practice.

Within groups of people performing contact improvisation, decisions about both artistic and organizational matters were most often made collectively, by consensus. People discussed an issue until agreement was reached, or until enough people relinquished their points of view. On the other hand, if no one was willing to make any decision, the person who finally spoke up prevailed.

Nancy Stark Smith described the situation which commonly arose within the ad hoc groups that collected on tour for any given performance. I quote her at length, because her statement so clearly presents the conflict between the ideology of "allowing things to happen" and the process of reaching a definitive decision:

> As time went on and more options became clear to people, it suddenly had to be decided how to present the contact. . . . One easy way to start had been to warm up and then find ourselves in a

"stand," do the small dance for a while, cool out the space. Who-
ever was ready first would just start moving and we'd all noodle
around for a while until a duet sort of took hold and then the
space would clear. We'd go on [with a round robin] until we felt
that it was finished and then we'd end.

After a while, we couldn't just do that anymore. We could if
we said, "Well, okay, let's start with a stand, and then go into a
round robin. . . ." But to say that is to take away the freedom to
change it. If it just happened that way, it was one thing, and if it
became habitual that it happened that way without saying anything was one thing, but to decide to make it that way was another.
So everybody's idea about improvisation, about performance,
about confidence [was raised]—and Steve was in his usual way very
ambiguous and hard to reach and would hardly commit himself to
anything.

So we were trying to practice this strange form of interper-
sonal, political contact improvisation in determining how to do
these performances. As usual, ambiguity reigned. . . . [It seemed
that] the person who wanted the most structure was the person
who was the least confident or . . . couldn't handle the freedom.
We'd go right up to a certain point and then five minutes before
performance, he'd say, "So we're going to start with a stand?" It's
like, how long can you stay in that ambiguous state? I'm not saying
that that was good or bad, but there definitely was that mood to it
and there would be that panic beforehand—someone would not
be able to handle the openness of it and would want to make structures. Finally, perhaps, those people decided, "Well, I'm going to
go make a contact performance and decide how I want the structure and get other people who do contact to do it." Sometimes
these contact groups that formed did so because they had a certain
affinity for a way of working and then that problem was somewhat
solved.

What seems obvious in Smith's account is that, as soon as dancers
moved beyond the demonstration mode of presenting contact improvisation, all the variables of improvisational performance, indeed of any
performance, surfaced. Paxton had intended contact improvisation to be
a clearly defined and limited structure so that all the issues of improvisation would not be raised and a particular area could be explored.
By confining the definition of contact to the physical give and take of

weight, the dance could be realized without any verbal exchange or additional decision-making, and participants could feel that it was allowed to happen. Smith adhered to this view when describing the person who can't "handle the freedom" and wants to make decisions consciously, in advance. Although her belief that anyone can do as she or he wishes also prompted her to add that she was not passing judgement, it seems evident that she preferred to avoid conscious decision-making.

Ideological prohibitions against making conscious decisions or "imposing" one's own beliefs on others are responsible to some degree for the lack of development of contact improvisation itself into a more frequently occurring performance form. This belief system conflicted with the need to make artistic decisions, so that attempts to direct pieces were often cut short by group dissension.[1] Only by the mid-'80s were dancers able to say easily that they were choreographing pieces for performance *and* doing contact improvisation.[2]

Using the structure of contact improvisation as a model for living did not always provide solutions to actual difficulties encountered in trying to maintain social organization either. The Ann Arbor contact community, which had supported classes, frequent jams, and several performing groups during the late '70s, dissolved for a few years in the early '80s before reforming again on a smaller scale. "People just didn't want to commit themselves any more to contact improvisation," one participant recalled. "It had been wonderful while it lasted, but we would have had to increase the involvement to go any further with it. People simply wanted to do other things." A dancer from a small contact community in a large city claimed that she left in the early '80s because the sense of obligation to the group was becoming oppressive: "I started not to like the dancing we were doing, and I was going to the jam every week because I felt I was supposed to, not because I wanted to."

The most active performing group, Mangrove, disbanded in 1980, existing for a brief time as Mangrove Productions and incorporating auxiliary members. With eight people in the group, Alan Ptashek suggested, decision-making was too difficult, and "people were losing a sense of themselves as individual artists." The social conditions of the '60s and

1. Free Lance Dance fell apart during its 1980 European tour over issues of giving and taking direction.

2. For example, Alito Alessi and Karen Nelson of Seattle collaboratively choreographed dances which were based on movements derived from contact improvisation and which also contained improvisational structures within them.

'70s had encouraged a conception of the individual which tied realization of individuality to a group; by the '80s, these conditions had virtually disappeared and the countercultural support for communal enterprises no longer existed. The underlying tensions between individual and group surfaced too powerfully to resist any longer.

Contact Improvisation as a Business

Other distinctions and questions arose within the contact improvisation movement as it expanded. For instance, the contact improvisation workshops in San Francisco held during the summers of 1976 and 1977 (called Focus) were "social events, a networking," at which different teachers joined together to present classes from which they made very little money. When, in 1978, Mangrove decided to organize their own summer workshop program, Focus did not materialize. "Other people were already starting to go off into their own work," said Alan Ptashek, "and Mangrove brought this to a head, left a gap. Their ambitions were raising issues: is contact improvisation a commercial, money-making venture?" Kris Wheeler also noted the eventual "division and factionalization" in the Bay Area. "There was a lot of generosity in the early years, with loose associations for performing. When Mangrove drew off to itself, others resented it." Mangrove dancer John LeFan defended his group, suggesting that he, for example, had a child to support and needed to make a living. "A lot of people were making money teaching and performing, but they didn't talk about it. Mangrove wasn't an exception, but it was well organized. We had good business people, and some other dancers were jealous."

California was not the only place where dancers discussed this question. Ellen Elias recalled "a lot of debate all over about the 'business' of Contact. Was it too mercenary to try to make a living from it?" The origins of contact improvisation had not been centered around establishing a dance company or school, and the early dancers had traveled and taught with little competition, often receiving grants or arranging jobs on the basis of Steve Paxton's reputation. As the movement expanded, participants articulated the ideology of cooperation, egalitarianism, and spontaneity. Many people who loved the dance form wanted to spend all their time doing it, yet that venture challenged their central ideology.

At times, the ideology was maintained. In 1976, for example, two management specialists tried to work with the most active contact impro-

visers, outlining plans in the *Contact Newsletter*. Ruth Carsch requested
information from all dancers, including résumés, public relations material, reviews, schedules of activities and future plans. She wrote: "From
a management and administrative point of view, *it is very important that
we tighten up 'Contact's' public image*. This can only be accomplished if we
centralize the managerial and administrative aspects of 'Contact'" (*Contact Newsletter* [Summer 1976]:4, emphasis in original). These plans never
materialized; dancers were not willing or able to organize themselves formally to the degree requested. In all probability, "tightening up" the public image through centralization would have greatly limited the spread of
contact improvisation engendered by its looseness and flexibility. At the
same time, it would have given contact improvisation a professional pro-
file which implicitly depends on exclusion of those who do not perform.

For several years, Roger Neece, a contact improviser from Boston
who was also interested in management and business, handled some of
the touring arrangements for East Coast dancers like Nancy Stark Smith
and Steve Paxton. Neece also helped form the nonprofit corporation
Contact Collaborations, Inc., in order to support *Contact Quarterly*. Neece
claimed he was always frustrated by the lack of business organization.
"Contact improvisation has never really been promoted," he said. "So
much more could be done from a business angle."

Many contact improvisers, particularly those without the reputation
of the more veteran dancers, had to confront the question of how to
build a reputation and make a living from dance. In 1978, Dena Davida,
then based in Montreal, wrote a letter to *Contact Quarterly* complaining
that she was beseiged by requests from touring dancers for sponsorship:

> I'm finding the cooperative philosophy turning into a show-biz
> type hustling. . . . PLEASE: take it easy. There is no fortune in this
> non-commercial form: touring can only mean adventure, learn-
> ing and good (crazy) times. . . . There are no rich producers, no
> standards of professionalism or commercial saleability as in the
> classic old model. So we make our own rules. . . . (*Contact Quarterly*
> 3[Winter 1978]:3)

Davida's warnings indicate her fear that contact improvisation would become like the rest of the performing dance world and her conviction that
the movement was trying to build alternative procedures. Yet participants found it hard to maintain alternatives in the context of that larger
dance world.

A description written by Jerry Zientara of the discussion "Business,

Survival, Contact Improvisation" at the 1980 American Dance Guild conference gives some idea of the demands placed on those who wished to operate in the dance world:

> Ellen Elias and Contactworks both described grant procedures necessary for operation. . . . There was a fair amount of talk about how to make Contact accessible to audiences, especially through lecture-demonstrations. How to sell ourselves and our work, where to look for buyers and how to approach them comprised an important section of the discussion. The importance of portfolio, brochure, letters of reference, publicity process, image and graphic design was stressed for performers/teachers who want to devote themselves professionally and full-time to art. Ability to deal with folks in terms of several vocabularies was pointed out as essential to make our form understood. The scale of investment necessary to conduct a business was also described in terms of phone bills, studio rental, travel expenses, and operating costs. Use of media for advertising, reviews and previews was also noted as part of the ongoing business. Professional contacters noted some feelings of resentment they had experienced from some contacters for whom the jam is a "free" practice, free certainly of business concerns. (1980)

People seeking to make a living from a dance form bring powerful influences to bear on it. For many contact improvisers in the late '70s, the thought of appealing to different audiences, winning grants, and defining their work for the dance marketplace conflicted with their experimental conception of the form. Ideologically, contact improvisation was supposed to demonstrate the artfulness of human behavior and interaction, which the audience was invited to share and observe. Dancers were to search for the unknown; as with any improvisational form, part of the intention of the work was to do something each time in a way in which it had never quite been done before. The contact improvisation movement thus had a product which was difficult to pin down. Its organization was also unsuitable for grant applications, because credit was communal and leadership implicit, whereas granting procedures usually demand evidence of a clearly identifiable, repeatable product, and of hierarchical structures which organize matters artistically and financially.

The problems presented by the business organization of contact improvisation dance companies mirror problems within other dance and arts organizations throughout this period, as well as conflicts experienced in other attempts at communal organization in the '60s and '70s. Katherine Newman, who researched the organization of twelve work collectives in California, found that "at the outset they did approximate their idealized view of an egalitarian distribution of authority" (1980:160). For the two collectives which were financially independent, the "original egalitarian format was maintained" even while "expanding their membership and enlarging the scope of their businesses. For the other ten collectives, however, the process of bureaucratization began at the point where they had to solicit outside support" (149). Newman concludes:

> Once the decision had been made to enter the "granting game," the collectives had to face an entirely different cultural milieu, one that rejected the value system which they espoused. The larger society and its institutions placed a positive value on hierarchy. The collectives had to contend with this clash in normative orientations from a rather weak position of financial dependency. Economic viability and cultural evaluation were intertwined difficulties that the collectives had to face. . . . (160–62)

The parallels within the contact improvisation movement to the work collectives are exemplified in the differences between Dance New England and dance companies based on contact improvisation. Dance New England, financially self-sufficient and self-contained as a social organization sponsoring a summer intensive workshop, has existed on a large scale since 1980 with an egalitarian, cooperative structure in which leadership and responsibility continuously rotate. The dance companies formed by contact improvisers, on the other hand, have had much greater difficulty maintaining their egalitarian organizations because they have had to become increasingly dependent on outside institutions such as granting agencies and the press for money and recognition. The pressures of these outside structures have often clashed with both the ideology and the organization of the contact improvisation dance companies.[3]

The disintegration of many contact improvisation dance companies and the split between amateur and professional in the early '80s can thus be attributed to intertwining artistic, social, and economic conditions.

3. In 1988, Channel Z, a collaborative improvisational company formed in 1983, suspended activity. Grant-giving agencies like the National Endowment for the Arts and the New York Foundation for the Arts do not accept applications from artists both as individuals and as members of a group. According to Nina Martin, the dancers in Channel Z, who were trying to develop both kinds of work, had to choose between them and finally decided to stop the collaboration for a while.

Some of the companies did not possess clear performance orientations, and many dancers did not have the skills or motivation required to extend contact improvisation into a performance art form when the public acceptance of less presentational showings waned. The ideology of "allowing the dance to happen" also mitigated against the development of what was often negatively perceived of as choreographic control. In addition, the technique itself became more refined, and distinctions between skilled and unskilled were more easily made, a development which contributed to the professionalization of performance for those who were capable of presenting the work more formally.

Social forces supporting the American counterculture also diminished, making collective endeavors more difficult. The collective nature of contact improvisation, which had been instrumental in its original formation, was no longer as viable ideologically. Changing social conditions and beliefs have been part of audience responses as well. Whereas early performances of contact improvisation commanded boisterous, exuberant attention from the audience, with viewers often jumping and rolling around after the presentation, later performances received more sedate, if warm, applause.[4] The two distinctive audience responses to contact improvisation indicate dramatic change—change which cannot be explained simply by observing alteration or development of movement techniques; they provide evidence of a shift in larger patterns of cultural values.

In addition, many participants in contact improvisation who had been students or young adults at the start of the '70s were approaching a different phase of their lives by the '80s. Certain accepted hallmarks of stability—marriage, children, careers—which had been rejected or postponed previously became more desirable as the years passed and people grew older. Moreover, the period of economic expansion in which that group of people could live marginally had ended. New people entering the form had come of age in another period and other economic circumstances, and they often held different values.

For example, Nina Martin, who danced in ad hoc performances of contact improvisation in the late '70s, began to choreograph evening-length concerts and to work with the improvisational dance group Channel Z in the mid-'80s. On the one hand, Martin subscribed to the older

4. Hervé Varenne (1986) has suggested that response constitutes the definition of a culturally significant utterance; the differences in audience responses to contact improvisation in the early '70s and the mid-'80s define the dancing differently in each time period.

ethos that anyone should be able to do contact improvisation with anyone else, and consequently, she refused to teach "advanced" classes. Everyone dancing together is "inherent to the beauty of the form," she said. On the other hand, she added, "Of course that doesn't mean you're going to perform with everybody," thus stating bluntly what was often left unsaid during developments in the late '70s.

In 1984, Martin also compared the past somewhat unfavorably with the present:

> In the hippie days, you saw the process at work, but there were elite groups watching, not the general public. Even when we'd perform in art galleries, for free, only a certain group of people came. The critics never reviewed our work. Now, Channel Z is a [*Village*] *Voice* Choice, critics come and review the work, and more people see what we're doing.

In this particular statement, Martin seems to view the former subculture of contact improvisation as isolating and to feel that legitimate forms of recognition, such as critical attention, signal a broader audience for the dancing. In a telling reversal, Martin felt she was being less "elitist" by participating in the legitimate structure of the dance world, the same reason given by the early contact improvisers for rejecting such a pursuit. In fact, both groups of dancers performed for a select group of people, not because the dancers were "elitist" in either case but because larger structures of education and occupation tend to circumscribe arts audiences.[5]

Bill T. Jones, at a public panel with Steve Paxton presented by the School for Movement Research in 1983, expressed a point of view related to Martin's in the comment above. Complaining about the "postmodernists" of the '60s and '70s, Jones asked:

> "How many of them have contributed to any of the major companies? How many of them have their PR [public relations] together,

5. Paul DiMaggio and Michael Useem (1983) have shown that from approximately 1960 to 1980, which is generally concurrent with the period of time in which the National Endowment for the Arts (founded in 1965) was mandated to fund artists and increase the arts audience, the composition of the audiences remained remarkably constant. "To summarize the unambiguous trends: the social composition of the arts audience is far more elite [meaning upper and upper-middle class] than the general public, and the center of the audience is more elite than its periphery. Education and, to a lesser degree, income are good predictors not only of who consumes the arts but of the intensity of their consumption" (217–18).

or their image together to get out and reach larger audiences, to really make a vital change in the scene? . . . Our generation, *my* generation, has been accused of being careerist, and I think that's because we hit the ground running; we saw the ground rules right off, and the seventies were over, you know, they cut us back [arts funding was cut], and we've got to get out there and compete with all the big cats, just so we can feed ourselves and continue making the work. So then you start thinking about things like repertory. Repertory's got to suit the ladies in Iowa and also the young intellectuals in downtown New York who write about you and help you get your reputation. . . ." (*Contact Quarterly* 9[Fall 1984]:36)

Jones's remarks reveal how economic considerations have a significant effect on creativity and the development of artistic work, considerations which have always permeated the American dance world but were largely ignored by the avant-garde throughout the '50s and '60s.[6] For many members of Jones and Martin's generation, rationales for participation in those social and economic structures that allow for money-making were based on conceptions about accessibility to a wide audience, exerting influence in the established dance world, and "realistically" building a career, that is, making a living from dancing. For Paxton and many of those who came of age in the '60s and early '70s, rationales for *not* participating actively in those structures were based on conceptions about researching new frontiers in movement, developing new social structures for making dance, and avoiding bureaucratic plans and organizational hierarchies which would interfere with the work and overtly conflict with its egalitarian and experimental premises. Over the years, opposition to the mainstream had been transformed into participating in the mainstream, a transformation characteristic of postmodernism (H. Foster 1985; Jameson 1983).

This contrast in rationales among dancers of different generations supports the proposal that periods in the life cycle of different generations, and the historical moments at which they came of age, are im-

6. Mary Overlie, the moderator of the panel, attempted to eliminate economics from the discussion, commenting, "I see a lot of concerns about money coming in, which I'd sort of like to shelve because it's not about work. . . ." On one level, Overlie may be correct that artists and audiences try to think only about "the work" when they discuss dance, leaving the economics of producing it aside. Yet obvious reasons existed for financial concerns to enter into the panel discussion: money influences artistic choices, and every dance artist must make decisions about his or her relationship to the social and economic structures which allow for money-making.

portant considerations in any discussion of cultural issues (Elder 1985). The contrasting rationales also point to contradictions in values and circumstances for both generations of dancers which are difficult to resolve satisfactorily. During the '6os, making dances and making a living could be thought of in separate categories—marginal living was both more economically feasible and more socially acceptable. In less expansive times, if one cannot make a living from dancing, then only the independently wealthy can pursue dance as a career for an extended period of time. However, if one must market one's work in order to make a living, that market exerts a powerful, often conservatizing influence on the dancing. Organizing dance comes to resemble a business and to require extensive resources. The long-standing belief in the American art tradition that the artist should respond to creative impulses without regard to "commercial" demands continues to conflict with the organizational necessity of presenting the art publicly.

Arts Organization and Postmodernism

The growth and decline of contact improvisation dance companies matched a national trend in dance companies of all kinds, reflecting national conditions for the performing arts. According to the National Endowment for the Arts, during the "'1960's and 1970's . . . new dance companies and choreographers came into being at frightening speed. . . . [In the late '70s] the numerical growth of new dance companies had started to level off . . . it is a very understandable response to the economics of the eighties'" (Sussmann 1984:23). Sociologist Leila Sussmann studied this trend and discovered that, although the number of dance companies increased rapidly in the '6os and '70s, the "turnover among them was also rapid; most dance companies had life spans of under five years. Among those still existing in 1980, the majority of modern companies were fewer than five years old and the majority of ballet companies were fewer than ten years old" (27). Contact improvisation dance companies were no exception to these national tendencies.

The government funding of the arts, which began in the '6os, had ramifications in dance organization which are still being realized. In 1964, the New York City Ballet received its first large grant from the Ford Foundation, and in 1965, the Congress established the National Endowment for the Arts. This funding led eventually to the creation of a small group of companies which could support choreographers and dancers at a marginal level year-round. While this support often required dancers to supplement their incomes by collecting unemployment a certain number of weeks a year, it enabled some people to dance full-time on a low but fairly steady income.

In addition to this group of "fully" employed, a much larger number of people were able to aspire to become choreographers or dancers, supporting themselves through small grants, teaching, and other part-time jobs (waiting tables or word-processing, for instance). Most of these choreographers have never been granted enough money to actually support dancers year-round, and most dancers have not held full-time employment. On the one hand, for the choreographers involved in making grant applications, government funding promoted the formation of "stable organizational structures with standard accounting procedures," a development which requires bureaucratization and rationalization of production (Peterson 1986:171; DiMaggio 1984). On the other hand, the situation has also contributed to a more ad hoc, dispersed method of training dancers and developing choreography: many people produce dances when the grant money is available and must disband their groups when the money runs out.

When Ronald Reagan's policies led to cuts in government arts funding in the early 1980s, many dance companies were caught with large organizational apparatuses which were difficult to maintain. Many collapsed. Those still in existence and those newly formed were forced into a fierce competition for limited funding and public support. This structure of production encouraged certain kinds of aesthetics, those which will "read" in big theaters and which can be sold to large audiences and bring in box office revenues. The comments by Nina Martin and Bill T. Jones quoted above reflect the reality of these conditions for the everyday life of artists.

Sociologist Richard Peterson has suggested that when arts administration becomes rationalized, it affects the art in two ways: different arts organizations in a discipline become more like each other, and, at the same time, "aesthetic fashions change more rapidly" (1986:179). Peterson's predictions match descriptions in the late '80s of many large-scale dance performances in America—ballet and modern dance styles merged, often on a superficial level, with many companies lacking stylistic distinctiveness, and audiences experienced difficulty discerning what the intention of the work might be. Simultaneously, artists often moved quickly in and out of critical favor.

A sociological perspective sheds additional light on what has happened to the experiments of the '60s in dance. Writers have often labeled

'6os dance as postmodern, identifying it with certain characteristics: fascination with the formal qualities of movement, an "anti-illusionist" stance, a self-reflexive or ironic attitude on the part of the performer, and a fragmentation or juxtaposition of styles, compositional devices, and narrative frameworks (Banes 1987; Johnston 1971, 1976). Yet the earnest pedestrianism and/or social commentary of work labeled post-modern in the '6os has been difficult to reconcile with the unabashed interest in spectacle and pastiche of work in the '8os labeled postmodern. A host of arguments and reworkings of the term, trying to arrive at a definition of postmodernism which will be applicable, has ensued.[7]

In the succeeding years, the experiments of the '6os in dance have developed within two kinds of organizational frameworks. One consists of small, often marginal social organizations—independent companies throughout the country, ad hoc performances, independent classes, courses within college dance departments, and social/teaching groups like Dance New England. A number of contact improvisers in fact have continued to work in this way, as have hundreds of American dancers of other aesthetic persuasions, many of them still engaged with ideas developed in the '6os. These dancers have seldom been cited as the post-modernists, because their work has not achieved the level of production demanded of funded dance in the '8os, the dance which most historians and critics have acknowledged.

The other development of experimental ideas has occurred in dance organizations which have gradually moved into a dance "mainstream," one that existed only in a very limited way prior to the '6os.[8] In the late '8os, "postmodernism" in dance lived alongside large, major ballet and traditional modern companies in a dance market that involved millions of dollars, and in a social organization that included not only the nonprofit dance corporations themselves but also large presenting organizations

7. See, for example, Sally Bane's introduction to the second edition of *Terpsichore in Sneakers* (1987) and Susan Manning's discussion of postmodernism in *The Drama Review* (1988). Also see Banes 1984; Daly 1987b; S. Foster 1986; Manning 1988; and the exchange between Banes and Manning (1989). Richard Schechner (1982) discusses the term "postmodernism" in relation to experimental theater; Hal Foster's (1983) collection of essays presents a range of opinions about the definition of postmodernism in the visual arts and architecture.

8. Experimental visual art, which is much more easily commodified than dance, vaulted quickly into a mainstream, postmodernist art world in the '6os. The visual artists connected with the Merce Cunningham Company and Judson Church—Jasper Johns, Robert Rauschenberg, Robert Morris—became much better known, earned far more money, and did so much more quickly than any of their most famous dance counterparts.

(such as the Brooklyn Academy of Music [BAM], City Center), corporate funding (Mobil, Philip Morris), powerful arts administrators and presenters (the director of BAM, the head of the National Endowment for the Arts), and the institutional apparatus of dance criticism in major newspapers and magazines.

Artistic ideas that at one point in history seemed alternative necessarily take on other meanings in a new context. This does not mean that innovative art cannot be presented in the Brooklyn Academy of Music, but what that innovation signifies to the audience which views it certainly remains open to question. The specific features of dance in and of themselves are difficult to identify as modernist or postmodernist, because further contextualization is needed to understand their meaning. "[E]ven if *all* the formal features [of postmodernism] were already present in the older high modernism," suggests cultural critic Fredric Jameson, "the very significance of those features changes when they become a cultural *dominant*, with a precise socioeconomic functionality" (1983:196). By the 1980s, perhaps for the first time in American history, avant-garde dance was being marketed as culturally dominant. To present something "new" was no longer antibourgeois; instead, "newness" constituted a selling point for a cultural product.

Contact Improvisation as American Culture

Dance occupies a peculiar position in American culture, at once marginal and compelling. The subject intrigues people, and some of their fascination results from a conception of dance as an exotic activity about which little is known and little can be known. This view is reinforced by the almost complete absence of reference to dance within the literature on American culture and art. Treatments of postmodernism in "all the arts" generally include literature, visual art, film, architecture, pop music, and new music, but not dance or theater (cf. Jameson 1983). The same might be said for feminist literature. Despite interest in the body, particularly the female body, feminist writers have never seriously considered the history of dance, particularly the remarkable circumstances of American modern dance, an art form largely developed by women.[9]

The marginalization of dance happens in all kinds of actions, ranging from the lack of cultural analysis of dance to the difficulty of making a

9. Feminist dance writers are the exception to this condition.

105. Nina Martin and Company in "Modern Daze" (1986). Benoit LeChambre escorts Martin over the backs of, *from left to right,* Teresa Reeves, Sharon Port, Margery Segal, Terry O'Reilly, Mary Overlie, and David Maier. Photo © 1986 by Dona Ann McAdams.

living as a dancer to the separation and fragmentation of kinds of dance in American culture. The position of dance contrasts with the prominent ritual and business of sports, particularly baseball and football, in American culture. Although many people are ignorant of sports, their lack of knowledge is an anomaly to be explained and defended, whereas ignorance of dance is commonplace and acceptable. American cultural values deem childhood participation in sports virtually mandatory for boys; childhood participation in dance is largely considered a pleasant, extracurricular activity for girls, a suspect activity for boys, and mandatory for neither sex. Those who speak about sports can talk about it in many ways—technically, sociologically, aesthetically. In education and in social activity, many different sports are practiced, and all are easily grouped as part of the same activity. The audience for sport crosses class, racial, and ethnic lines, just as its participants do. It is no wonder that American dancers and audiences are aesthetically influenced by athletics; sport is our most prominent visual referent for physical skill.

106. Dena Davida, *left*, and Louise Parent in "Pièce de Résistance" (1986).
Photo © 1986 by Ormsby K. Ford.

But dance also has powerful features residing in its difference from sport. Dance, as a primarily social and aesthetic activity in America, engages people in actions associated with creativity, expression, identity, and spirituality in movement. Dance is difficult to mass market and to commodify because it depends on live performance and oral and kinesthetic transmission. Thus its strengths lie in local participation, in the dancing which happens in particular places on particular occasions, both social and theatrical. Contact improvisation, insofar as it has succeeded in generating different kinds of dance communities and practices, offers one model for how dance can flourish and proliferate in American culture. The point is not that everyone should do contact improvisation, but that access to dance of some kind might be recognized and created in more circumstances than currently exist.

Understanding dance in America requires an understanding of the intertwining of social life and aesthetic concepts. Contact improvisation, as the embodiment of a political period, the '60s, reveals a certain legacy. It signifies the struggle throughout the '60s to create alternative organizations for dance, both socially and artistically, in the midst of a society that generally rewards people only for individual action. The difficulties encountered attest to the power of social structures to limit cultural invention, but the experiences which were and are being created continue to hold forth other possibilities.

Contact improvisation also constituted one part of a larger cultural preoccupation with the body emerging in the '60s, evident in theater dance of all sorts, in "physical" theater, in American social dance, in psychological movements, and in the "sexual revolution." "Body" became something to be experienced "from the inside," seen to represent and create a sense of self that was sensual, physical, and physically intelligent. This body is now a cultural concept manifest in many kinds of artistic, athletic, educational, and therapeutic practices.

These ideas existed before the '60s, and they have never achieved cultural hegemony. But this conception of body on which they are based became a significant part of everyday practices in certain realms of the culture in the '60s and continues today. Interest in sports, aerobics, fitness, and body therapy are to some degree part of that legacy, however it might be distorted or enhanced in particular circumstances. The possibility that people could fall in love with contact improvisation did not exist before the '60s, not just because contact improvisation hadn't been invented—in fact, many dancers had played with partnering, with ways

107. Unidentified contact improvisers in Montreal. Photo © 1986 by Harold Vaselin.

108. Members of Channel Z performing in 1986. *From left to right,* Paul Langland, Randy Warshaw, and Diane Madden. Photo © 1986 by Dona Ann McAdams.

109. Karen Nelson and Alito Alessi in "Hoop Dance" (1988). Photo © 1988 by Cliff Coles.

to lift and carry, and with improvisation—but also because the conception of the body which underlies such a dance form had not yet become a widespread cultural idea.

In one sense, it can be said that contact improvisation was of the moment for only a moment, in the early years of its development, and that it crested at the same time that its social bases were being fatally eroded. Thus viewed, the "story" of contact improvisation is a story about the end of the '60s.

Yet contact improvisation continues to exist. Hundreds of people currently study and practice the form. New national meetings have developed; the Breiten Beach jam, for example, started in 1980 by Karen Nelson and Alito Alessi, continues to meet annually, attended (and sold out weeks in advance) by dancers from all over the country. Performance activity waxes and wanes, springing up again in new locations and, with each performance, presenting contact improvisation to some people for the first time. Teaching contact improvisation remains a steady practice. Active contact improvisation centers have now developed in Europe (for example, in France, Germany, the Netherlands, Italy, Belgium), where dancers have held annual international contact improvisation teaching/ performing conferences since 1984.

On a larger level, then, contact improvisation has made significant contributions to American modern dance and continues to provide a distinctive body image and movement experience for those who do it and watch it. The historical record of its development informs us about the problems and possibilities of change in American culture and about the influence of national economic and social institutions and values on artistic experimentation. Contact improvisation demonstrates how dance is a part of life and culture—as metaphor for social interaction and values, as a focal point for different kinds of organizations and institutions, and, not least of all, as the direct apprehension of moving with and for a community of people. In the moment of dancing, people experience powerful occasions of meaning in their lives.

References
Index

References

Books and Articles

Alexander, F. Matthias. 1969. *The Philosophy of the Body*. New York: University Books.

Arensberg, Conrad, and Solon Kimball. 1965. *Culture and Community*. New York: Harcourt, Brace and World.

Artaud, Antonin. 1958. *The Theater and Its Double*. Trans. Mary Carolina Richards. New York: Grove Press Inc.

Banes, Sally. 1984. *Democracy's Body*. Ann Arbor, Michigan: UMI Research Press.

Banes, Sally. 1987. *Terpsichore in Sneakers*. 2nd ed. New York: Houghton Mifflin.

Banes, Sally, and Susan Manning. 1989. Letters. *The Drama Review* 121 (Spring): 13–16.

Bartenieff, Irmgard, with Dori Lewis. 1980. *Body Movement: Coping with the Environment*. New York: Gordon and Breach.

Barthes, Roland. 1972. *Mythologies*. New York: Hill and Wang.

Beck, Julian. 1972. *The Life of the Theatre: The Relation of the Artist to the Struggle of the People*. San Francisco: City Lights.

Becker, Howard S. 1982. *Art Worlds*. Berkeley: University of California Press.

Bellah, Robert N., et al. 1985. *Habits of the Heart: Individualism and Commitment in American Life*. New York: Harper and Row, Publishers.

Belo, Jane. 1970. "The Balinese Temper." In Jane Belo, ed., *Traditional Balinese Culture*, pp. 85–110. New York: Columbia University Press.

Belz, Carl. 1972. *The Story of Rock*. New York: Oxford University Press.

Bensman, Joseph. 1983. "Introduction: The Phenomenology and Sociology of the Performing Arts." In Jack Kamerman and Rosanne Martorella, eds., *Performers and Performances. The Social Organization of Artistic Work*, pp. 1–38. New York: Praeger Publishers.

Bentley, Toni. 1982. *Winter Season*. New York: Vintage Books.

Birdwhistell, Ray L. 1970. *Kinesics and Context*. Philadelphia: University of Pennsylvania Press.

Blacking, John, ed. 1977. *The Anthropology of the Body*. New York: Academic Press, Inc.

Blacking, John, and Kealiinohomoku, Joann, eds. 1979. *The Performing Arts. Music and Dance*. New York: Mouton Publishers.

Bloch, Maurice. 1986. *From Blessing to Violence*. Cambridge: Cambridge University Press.

Boaz, Franziska. 1944. *The Function of Dance in Human Society*. New York: Dance Horizons.

Booth, Laurie. 1980. "Mangrove at Jackson's Lane and the Place." *New Dance* 16:16.

Bourdieu, Pierre. 1984. *Distinction: A Social Critique of the Judgement of Taste*. Trans. Richard Nice. Cambridge: Harvard University Press.

Brook, Peter. 1968. *The Empty Space*. New York: Atheneum Press.

Brown, Beverly. 1971–72. "Training to Dance with Erick Hawkins." *Dance Scope* 12(2):6–30.

Brown, Carolyn, et al. 1968. "Time to Walk in Space" (essays on Merce Cunningham). *Dance Perspectives* 34 (Summer).

Brown, Jean Morrison, ed. 1979. *The Vision of Modern Dance*. Princeton, New Jersey: Princeton Book Company, Publishers.

Bull, Richard. 1969. "On Structural Improvisation." *Focus on Dance* 5:49–50.

Bull, Richard, ed. 1967. *Research in Dance: Problems and Possibilities*. New York: CORD.

Cage, John. 1966. *Silence*. Cambridge: Massachusetts Institute of Technology.

Caplan, Pat, ed. 1987. *The Cultural Construction of Sexuality*. London and New York: Tavistock Publications.

Campbell, Charles. 1980. "Mangrove." *New Dance* 14:6.

Chernoff, John. 1983. *African Rhythm and African Sensibility: Aesthetics and Social Action in African Musical Idioms*. Chicago: University of Chicago Press.

Clark, Barbara. 1975. *Body Proportion Needs Depth*. Urbana, Illinois: Barbara Clark.

Clarke, Mary, and Quentin Crisp. 1982. *The History of Dance*. New York: Crown Publishers.

Clifford, James. 1983. "On Anthropological Authority." *Representations* 2:132–43.

Clifford, James. 1988. *The Predicament of Culture: Twentieth-Century Ethnography, Literature, and Art*. Cambridge: Harvard University Press.

Clifford, James, and George Marcus, eds. 1986. *Writing Culture: The Poetics and Politics of Ethnography*. Berkeley: University of California Press.

Cohen, Selma Jeanne. 1965. *The Modern Dance: Seven Statements of Belief*. Middletown, Connecticut: Wesleyan University Press.

Cohen, Selma Jeanne. 1972. *Doris Humphrey: An Artist First*. Middletown, Connecticut: Wesleyan University Press.

Cohn, Nik. 1969. *Rock from the Beginning*. New York: Stein and Day.

Contact Newsletter. 1975–76, Nos. 1–4.

Contact Quarterly. 1976–88, Vols. 1–13.

Cope, Edith. 1976. *Performances: Dynamics of a Dance Group*. London: Lepus Books.

Copeland, Roger, and Marshall Cohen, eds. 1983. *What Is Dance? Readings in Theory and Criticism*. New York: Oxford University Press.

Cunningham, Merce. 1968. *Changes*. New York: Something Else Press.

Cunningham, Merce. 1985. *The Dancer and the Dance. Merce Cunningham in Conversation with Jacqueline Lesschaeve*. New York: M. Boyars Publishers.

Daly, Ann. 1987a. "The Balanchine Woman: Of Hummingbirds and Channel Swimmers." *The Drama Review* 31(1):8–21.

Daly, Ann. 1987b. "BAM and Beyond: The Postmoderns Get Balleticized." *High Performance* 38:46–49.

Daly, Ann. 1987–88. "Classical Ballet: A Discourse of Difference." *Women and Performance, A Journal of Feminist Theory* 3(2):57–66.

Daniel, Ana. 1981. *Bali, Behind the Mask*. New York: Alfred A. Knopf.

Darnton, Robert. 1984. *The Great Cat Massacre, and Other Episodes in French Cultural History*. New York: Basic Books, Inc.

Darwin, Charles. 1965. *The Expression of the Emotions in Man and Animals*. Chicago: University of Chicago Press.

Dell, Cecily. 1977. *A Primer for Movement Description*. New York: Dance Notation Bureau Press.

Dickstein, Morris. 1977. *Gates of Eden: American Culture in the Sixties*. New York: Basic Books, Inc.

DiMaggio, Paul J. 1984. "The Nonprofit Instrument and the Influence of the Marketplace on Policies in the Arts." In W. McNeil Lowry, ed., *The Arts and Public Policy in the United States*, pp. 57–99. Englewood Cliffs, New Jersey: Prentice-Hall, Inc.

DiMaggio, Paul J., ed. 1986. *Nonprofit Enterprise in the Arts*. New York and Oxford: Oxford University Press.

DiMaggio, Paul, and Michael Useem. 1983. "Cultural Democracy in a Period of Cultural Expansion: The Social Composition of Arts Audiences in the United States." In Jack Kamerman and Rosanne Martorella, eds., *Performers and Performances: The Social Organization of Artistic Work*, pp. 199–226. New York: Praeger Publishers.

Dolgin, J. L., D. S. Kemnitzer, and D. M. Schneider, eds. 1977. *Symbolic Anthropology*. New York: Columbia University Press.

Douglas, Mary. 1982. *Natural Symbols*. New York: Pantheon Books.

Douglas, Mary, ed. 1973. *Rules and Meanings*. Middlesex, England: Penguin Education.

Dumont, Louis. 1966. *Homo Hierarchicus*. Chicago: University of Chicago Press.

Durkheim, Emile, and Marcel Mauss. 1963. *Primitive Classification*. Trans. Rodney Needham. Chicago: University of Chicago Press.

Egan, Gerard, ed. 1971. *Encounter Groups*. Belmont, California: Brooks Cole Publishing Company.

Ekman, Paul. 1980. *The Faces of Man*. New York: Garland Publishing, Inc.

Elder, G., Jr. 1985. *Life Course Dynamics: Trajectories and Transitions, 1968–1980*. Ithaca, New York: Cornell University Press.

Elias, Ellen. 1978. "Erick Hawkins: Sensation, Effortlessness, Technique." *Eddy* 10:31–33.

Emery, Lynne Fauley. 1972. *Black Dance in the United States from 1619 to 1970.* Palo Alto, California: National Press Books.

Feld, Steven. 1982. *Sound and Sentiment.* Philadelphia: University of Pennsylvania Press.

Feldenkrais, Moshe. 1972. *Awareness Through Movement.* New York: Harper and Row, Publishers.

Firth, Raymond. 1973. *Symbols: Public and Private.* Ithaca, New York: Cornell University Press.

Fisher, Seymour. 1972. "Body Image" in David Sills, ed., *International Encyclopedia of the Social Sciences*, Vol. 2, pp. 113–16. New York: Macmillan.

Fishwick, Marshall, and R. B. Browne, eds. 1970. *Icons of Popular Culture.* Bowling Green, Ohio: Bowling Green University Press.

Forti, Simone. 1974. *Handbook in Motion.* New York: New York University Press.

Foster, Hal. 1985. *Recodings: Art, Spectacle, Cultural Politics.* Port Townsend, Washington: Bay Press.

Foster, Hal, ed. 1983. *The Anti-Aesthetic: Essays in Post-Modern Culture.* Port Townsend, Washington: Bay Press.

Foster, Susan. 1986. *Reading Dancing: Bodies and Subjects in Contemporary American Dance.* Berkeley: University of California Press.

Frith, Simon. 1984. "Rock and the Politics of Memory." In Sohnya Sayres et al., ed., *The 60s Without Apology*, pp. 59–69. Minneapolis: University of Minnesota in cooperation with *Social Text*.

Furse, Anna. 1981. "From Outside In to Inside Out." *New Dance* 17:9–11.

Geertz, Clifford. 1973. *The Interpretation of Cultures.* New York: Basic Books, Inc.

Geertz, Clifford. 1977. "'From the Native's Point of View': On the Nature of Anthropological Understanding." In J. L. Dolgin, D. S. Kemnitzer, and D. M. Schneider, eds., *Symbolic Anthropology*, pp. 480–92. New York: Columbia University Press.

Geertz, Clifford. 1983. *Local Knowledge.* New York: Basic Books, Inc.

Glassie, Henry. 1970. "Artifacts: Folk, Popular, Imaginary and Real." In Marshall Fishwick and R. B. Browne, eds., *Icons of Popular Culture.* pp. 103–22. Bowling Green, Ohio: Bowling Green University Press.

Glassie, Henry. 1977. "Meaningful Things and Appropriate Myths. The Artifact's Place in American Studies." *Prospects: An Annual of American Cultural Studies* 3:1–49.

Goffman, Erving. 1976. *Gender Advertisements.* New York: Harper and Row, Publishers.

Graff, Ellen. 1985. "Contact Improvisation: The Dance Utopia of Steve Paxton." Unpublished manuscript; available from Graff.

Green, Harvey. 1986. *Fit for America. Health, Fitness, Sport and American Society.* New York: Pantheon Books.

Grotowski, Jerzy. 1968. *Towards a Poor Theatre.* New York: Simon and Schuster.

Hall, Edward T. 1969. *The Hidden Dimension.* Garden City, New York: Doubleday and Company, Inc.

Halprin, Anna. 1957. "Intuition and Improvisation" in Marian van Tuyl, ed. *Anthology of Impulse.* pp. 50–53. Brooklyn, New York: Dance Horizons.

Halprin, Anna. 1965. "Yvonne Rainer Interviews Anna Halprin." *The Drama Review* 10:168–78.

Halprin, Anna. 1967–68. "The Process is the Purpose: An Interview by Vera Maletic." *Dance Scope* 4(1):11–18.

Halprin, Anna. 1980. Address to the American Dance Guild. 19 June.

Hanna, Judith Lynne. 1987. *To Dance Is Human: A Theory of Non-Verbal Communication.* 2nd ed. Chicago: University of Chicago Press.

Hartman, Rose. 1977–78. "Talking with Anna Halprin." *Dance Scope* 12(1):57–66.

Hawkins, Erick. 1965. "Pure Poetry." In Selma Jeanne Cohen, ed., *The Modern Dance: Seven Statements of Belief*, pp. 39–58. Middletown, Connecticut: Wesleyan University Press.

Henley, Nancy. 1977. *Body Politics.* Englewood Cliffs, New Jersey: Prentice-Hall, Inc.

Herrigel, Eugen. 1953. *Zen in the Art of Archery.* New York: Pantheon Books, Inc.

Holroyde, Peggy. 1972. *The Music of India.* New York: Praeger Publishers.

Humphrey, Doris. 1970. "America's Modern Dance." In Myron Howard Nadel and Constance Gwen Nadel, eds., *The Dance Experience*, pp. 105–9. New York: Praeger Publishers.

Jameson, Fredric. 1983. "Postmodernism, or the Cultural Logic of Late Capitalism." *New Left Review* 146:53–92.

Jameson, Fredric. 1984. "Periodizing the 60s." In Sohnya Sayres et al., *The 60s Without Apology*, pp. 178–215. Minneapolis: University of Minnesota Press in cooperation with *Social Text.*

Johnston, Jill. 1971. *Marmalade Me.* New York: E. P. Dutton and Co., Inc.

Johnston, Jill. 1976. "The New American Modern Dance." *Salmagundi* 33–34: 149–74.

Jowitt, Deborah. 1977. "Fall, You Will be Caught." *Village Voice* (5 September).

Jowitt, Deborah. 1988. *Time and the Dancing Image.* New York: William Morrow and Co.

Kaeppler, Adrienne. 1978. "Dance in Anthropological Perspective." *Annual Review of Anthropology* 7:31–49.

Kaeppler, Adrienne. 1985. "Structured Movement Systems in Tonga." In Paul Spencer, ed., *Society and the Dance: The Social Anthropology of Process and Performance*, pp. 92–118. Cambridge: Cambridge University Press.

Kagan, Elizabeth, and Margaret Morse. 1988. "The Body Electronic: Aerobic Exercise on Video—Women's Search for Empowerment and Self-Transformation." *The Drama Review* 120(Winter):164–80.

Kamerman, Jack B., and Rosanne Martorella, eds. 1983. *Performers and Performances. The Social Organization of Artistic Work.* New York: Praeger Publishers.

Kealiinohomoku, Joann. 1969. "An Anthropologist Looks at Ballet as a Form of Ethnic Dance." *Impulse* 20:24–33.

Kealiinohomoku, Joann. 1974. "Caveat on Causes and Correlations." *CORD News* 6(2):20–24.

Kealiinohomoku, Joann. 1976. "Theory and Methods for an Anthropological Study of Dance." Ph.D. dissertation, Indiana University.

Kendall, Elizabeth. 1979. *Where She Danced*. New York: Alfred A. Knopf.

Kirby, Michael. 1969. *The Art of Time: Essays on the Avant-Garde*. New York: E. P. Dutton and Co.

Kirby, Michael, ed. 1965. *Happenings*. New York: E. P. Dutton and Co.

Klosty, James, ed. 1975. *Merce Cunningham*. New York: E. P. Dutton and Co.

Kostelanetz, Richard. 1970. "Metamorphosis in Modern Dance." *Dance Scope* 5(1):6–21.

Kreemer, Connie. 1987. *Further Steps: 15 Choreographers on Modern Dance*. New York: Harper and Row, Publishers.

Laban, Rudolf. 1971. *The Mastery of Movement*. 3rd ed. rev. and enl. by Lisa Ullmann. Boston: Plays, Inc.

Laban, Rudolf. 1974. *The Language of Movement: A Guidebook to Choreutics*. Annotated and ed. by Lisa Ullmann. Boston: Plays, Inc.

La Barre, Weston. 1980. *Culture in Context*, "Paralinguistics, Kinesics, and Cultural Anthropology," pp. 289–332. Durham, North Carolina: Duke University Press.

Laine, Barry. 1983. "Is Contact Improvisation Really Dance?" *New York Times*, 3 July, pp. 7H and 12H.

Layton, Robert. 1981. *The Anthropology of Art*. New York: Columbia University Press.

Leach, Edmund. 1961. *Rethinking Anthropology*. New York: Humanities Press, Inc.

Leatherman, LeRoy. 1966. *Martha Graham: Portrait of the Lady as an Artist*. New York: Alfred A. Knopf.

Lepczyk, Billie Frances. 1981. "A Contrastive Study of Movement Style in Dance through the Laban Perspective." Ph.D. dissertation, Teacher's College, Columbia University.

Levinson, André. (1918) 1985. *Ballet Old and New*. Translated by Susan Cook Sumner. Brooklyn, New York: Dance Horizons.

Lévi-Strauss, Claude. 1966. *The Savage Mind*. Chicago: University of Chicago Press.

Lévi-Strauss, Claude. 1967. *Structural Anthropology*. Trans. Claire Jacobson and Brooke Grundfest Schoepf. Garden City, New York: Doubleday and Company, Inc.

Lévi-Strauss, Claude. 1975. *The Raw and the Cooked*. Trans. John and Doreen Weightman. New York: Harper Colophon Books.

Liebow, Elliot. 1967. *Tally's Corner*. Boston: Little, Brown and Company.

Lomax, Alan. 1968. *Folk Song Style and Culture*. Washington, D.C.: American Association for the Advancement of Science.

Lowry, W. McNeil, ed. 1984. *The Arts and Public Policy in the United States*. Englewood Cliffs, New Jersey: Prentice-Hall, Inc.

Luger, Eleanor Rachel. 1977. "Contact Improvisation." *Dance Magazine*: 41–43.

Luger, Eleanor Rachel. 1977–78. "A Contact Improvisation Primer." *Dance Scope* 12(1):48–56.

McClellan, Tara. 1980. "Contact Improvisation." Unpublished manuscript; available from McClellan.

McDermott, Jane. 1977. "An Interview with Steve Paxton." *New Dance* 4:5–8.

Malina, Judith, and Julian Beck. 1971. *Paradise Now*. New York: Random House.

Manning, Susan Allene. 1987. "Body Politic: The Dances of Mary Wigman." Ph.D. dissertation, Columbia University.

Manning, Susan. 1988. "Modernist Dogma and 'Post-Modern' Rhetoric: A Response to Sally Banes' *Terpsichore in Sneakers.*" *The Drama Review* 120(Winter): 32–39.

Marcus, George F., and Dick Cushman. 1982. "Ethnographies as Text." *Annual Review of Anthropology* 11:25–69.

Marcus, George F., and Michael M. J. Fischer. 1986. *Anthropology as Cultural Critique: An Experimental Moment in the Human Sciences*. Chicago: University of Chicago Press.

Martin, John. 1968. *The Modern Dance*. Reprint ed. Brooklyn, New York: Dance Horizons.

Marx, Karl. 1965. *The German Ideology*. New York: International Publishers.

Marx, Leo. 1964. *The Machine in the Garden: Technology and the Pastoral Ideal in America*. New York: Oxford University Press.

Matheson, Katy. Forthcoming 1991. "Improvisation." In Selma Jeanne Cohen, ed., *International Encyclopedia of Dance*. Berkeley: University of California Press.

Mauss, Marcel. 1973. "Techniques of the Body." *Economy and Society* 2:70–87.

Mead, Margaret, and Frances Cooke Macgregor. 1951. *Growth and Culture*. New York: G. P. Putnam's Sons.

Meyer, Leonard B. 1965. *Music, the Arts, and Ideas*. Chicago: University of Chicago Press.

Morrison, Jack. 1973. *The Rise of the Arts on the American Campus*. New York: McGraw-Hill Book Company.

Murphy, Robert F. 1971. *The Dialectics of Social Life: Alarms and Excursions in Anthropological Theory*. New York: Columbia University Press.

Murphy, Robert F. 1987. *The Body Silent*. New York: Henry Holt and Company.

Newman, Katherine. 1980. "Incipient Bureaucracy: The Development of Hierarchies in Egalitarian Organizations." In Gerald M. Britan and Ronald Cohen, eds., *Hierarchy and Society*, pp. 143–63. Philadelphia: Institute for the Study of Human Issues.

Nketia, J. H. Kwabena. 1974. *The Music of Africa*. New York: W. W. Norton and Co., Inc.

Novack, Cynthia. 1984. "Ethnography and History: A Case Study of a Conference of Dance Improvisers." In Christina Schlundt, ed., *Proceedings of the Society of Dance History Scholars*. pp. 1–9. University of California, Davis.

Novack, Cynthia. 1986. "Sharing the Dance: An Ethnography of Contact Improvisation." Ph.D. dissertation, Columbia University.

Novack, Cynthia. 1988a. "Looking at Movement as Culture." *The Drama Review* 120(Winter):102–19.

Novack, Cynthia. 1988b. "Contact Improvisation: Photo Essay and Summary Movement Analysis." *The Drama Review* 120(Winter):120–34.

Novack, Cynthia. Forthcoming 1991. "Ritual and Dance." In Selma Jeanne Cohen, ed., *International Encyclopedia of Dance*. Berkeley: University of California Press.

O'Neill, John. 1985. *Five Bodies: The Human Shape of Modern Society*. Ithaca, New York: Cornell University Press.

Paxton, Steve. 1971. "The Grand Union." *The Drama Review* 16:128–34.

Paxton, Steve. 1975. "Contact Improvisation." *The Drama Review* 19(1):40–42.

Paxton, Steve. 1980. Keynote address. American Dance Guild Annual Meeting, Minneapolis, Minnesota, 16 June.

Paxton, Steve. 1981–82. "Contact Improvisation." *Theatre Papers, The Fourth Series* (Dartingon, England).

Peacock, James. 1968. *Rites of Modernization: Symbolic and Social Aspects of Indonesian Proletarian Drama*. Chicago: University of Chicago Press.

Pennella, Florence. 1978. "The Vision of Erick Hawkins." *Dance Scope* 12(2): 14–23.

Peterson, Richard A. 1986. "From Impresario to Arts Administrator: Formal Accountability in Nonprofit Cultural Organizations." In Paul J. DiMaggio, ed., *Nonprofit Enterprise in the Arts*, pp. 161–83. New York, Oxford: Oxford University Press.

Peterson, Richard A., ed. 1976. *The Production of Culture*. Beverly Hills, London: Sage Publications.

Pierpont, Margaret. 1980. "America on the Move: Summerdance 1980." *Dance Magazine* (September):80–81.

Rainer, Yvonne. 1974. *Work 1961–1973*. New York: New York University Press.

Rainer, Yvonne. 1984. Lecture. School for Movement Research, New York City, 16 May.

Real, Michael R. 1977. *Mass-Mediated Culture*. Englewood Cliffs, New Jersey: Prentice-Hall, Inc.

Royce, Anya Peterson. 1977. *The Anthropology of Dance*. Bloomington: Indiana University Press.

Ruyter, Nancy L. C. 1979. *Reformers and Visionaries, the Americanization of the Art of Dance*. New York: Dance Horizons.

Ryan, Peter. 1980. "Dance as Art-Sport." *Vandance* 9(1):8–9.

Sachs, Curt. 1963. *World History of the Dance*. Trans. Bessie Schoenberg. New York: W. W. Norton and Co., Inc.

Sahlins, Marshall. 1976. *Culture and Practical Reason*. Chicago: University of Chicago Press.

Sahlins, Marshall. 1981. *Historical Metaphors and Mythical Realities*. Ann Arbor: University of Michigan Press.

Sahlins, Marshall. 1985. *Islands of History*. Chicago: University of Chicago Press.

Sayres, Sohnya, et al. 1984. *The 60s Without Apology*. Minneapolis: University of Minnesota Press in cooperation with *Social Text*.

Schechner, Richard. 1970. *Dionysus in '69*. New York: Farrar, Straus & Giroux.

Schechner, Richard. 1973. *Environmental Theater*. New York: Hawthorn.

Schechner, Richard. 1982. *The End of Humanism*. New York: Performing Arts Journal Publications.

Schechner, Richard, and Mady Schuman, eds. 1976. *Ritual, Play, and Performance*. New York: Seabury Press.

Scheflen, Albert E. 1972. *Body Language and Social Order*. Englewood Cliffs, New Jersey: Prentice-Hall, Inc.

Schieffelin, Edward. 1976. *The Sorrow of the Lonely and the Burning of the Dancers*. New York: St. Martin's Press.

Schneider, David M. 1980. *American Kinship: A Cultural Account*. 2nd ed. Chicago: University of Chicago Press.

Shelton, Suzanne. 1981. *Divine Dancer, the Biography of Ruth St. Denis*. Garden City, New York: Doubleday and Co., Inc.

Siegel, Marcia B. 1971. "Nik, a Documentary." *Dance Perspectives* 48.

Siegel, Marcia B. 1979. *The Shapes of Change*. Boston: Houghton Mifflin.

Siegel, Marcia B. 1988. *Days on Earth: The Dance of Doris Humphrey*. New Haven and London: Yale University Press.

Singer, Milton. 1972. *When a Great Tradition Modernizes. An Anthropological Approach to Indian Civilization*. Chicago: University of Chicago Press.

Spencer, Paul, ed. 1985. *Society and the Dance: The Social Anthropology of Process and Performance*. Cambridge: Cambridge University Press.

Spindler, George, and Louise Spindler. 1983. "Anthropologists View American Culture." In *Annual Reviews in Anthropology* 12:49–78. Palo Alto, California: Annual Reviews.

Stearns, Marshall, and Jean Stearns. 1968. *Jazz Dance: The Story of American Vernacular Dance*. New York: Macmillan.

Steinman, Louise. 1986. *The Knowing Body*. Boston: Shambhala.

Stodelle, Ernestine. 1978. *The Dance Technique of Doris Humphrey*. Princeton, New Jersey: Princeton Book Company, Publishers.

Stodelle, Ernestine. 1984. *Deep Song: The Dance Story of Martha Graham*. New York: Schirmer Books.

"The Studies Project." 1983. School for Movement Research, New York City, 4 December. Transcript in *Contact Quarterly* 9(Fall 1984):30–37.

Susman, Warren. 1984. *Culture as History*. New York: Pantheon Books.

Sussmann, Leila. 1984. "Anatomy of the Dance Company Boom, 1958–1980." *Dance Research Journal* 16(2):23–28.

Sweet, Jill D. 1985. *Dances of the Tewa Pueblo Indians*. Santa Fe: School of American Research.

Sweigard, Lulu. 1974. *Human Movement Potential: Its Ideokinetic Facilitation*. New York: Dodd, Mead and Company.

Taylor, Paul. 1987. *Private Domain*. New York: Alfred A. Knopf.

Thompson, Robert Farris. 1963. *African Art in Motion: Icon and Act*. Berkeley: University of California Press.

Thompson, Robert Farris. 1983. *Flash of the Spirit: African and Afro-American Art and Philosophy*. New York: Random House.

Todd, Mabel Ellsworth. [1937] 1972. *The Thinking Body*. Brooklyn, New York: Dance Horizons.

Tomkins, Calvin. 1965. *The Bride and the Bachelors*. New York: Viking Press.

Tomkins, Calvin. 1980. *Off the Wall: Robert Rauschenberg and the Art of Our Times*. New York: Penguin Books.

Turner, Victor. 1967. *The Forest of Symbols, Aspects of Ndembu Ritual*. Ithaca, New York: Cornell University Press.

Turner, Victor. 1969. *The Ritual Process: Structure and Anti-Structure*. Chicago: Aldine.

Turner, Victor. 1974. *Dramas, Fields, and Metaphors*. Ithaca, New York: Cornell University Press.

Ueshiba, Kisshomaru. 1984. *The Spirit of Aikido*. Trans. Taitetsu Unno. New York: Kodansha International.

Varenne, Hervé. 1977. *Americans Together: Structured Diversity in a Midwestern Town*. New York: Teachers College Press.

Varenne, Hervé, ed. 1986. *Symbolizing America*. Lincoln: University of Nebraska Press.

Vatsyayan, Kapila. 1968. *Classical Indian Dance in Literature and the Arts*. New Delhi: Sangeet Natak Akademi.

Vaughn, David, et al. 1987. "Cunningham and His Dancers." *Ballet Review* 15(3): 19–40.

Vidich, Arthur, and Joseph Bensman. 1968. *Small Towns and Mass Society*. Princeton, New Jersey: Princeton University Press.

Warner, W. Lloyd. 1941–59. *Yankee City Series*. New Haven: Yale University Press.

Weber, Max. 1967. *From Max Weber: Essays in Sociology*. Trans. H. H. Gerth and C. Wright Mills. New York: Oxford University Press.

White, Hayden. 1973. *Metahistory: The Historical Imagination in Nineteenth Century Europe*. Baltimore: Johns Hopkins University Press.

Whyte, William. 1966. *Street Corner Society*. Chicago: University of Chicago Press.

Williams, Raymond. 1959. *Culture and Society, 1880–1950*. Garden City, New York: Doubleday and Co., Inc.

Williams, Raymond. 1976. *Keywords, A Vocabulary of Culture and Society*. New York: Oxford University Press.

Williams, Raymond. 1982. *The Sociology of Culture*. New York: Schocken Books.

Wright, Will. 1977. *Sixguns and Society, A Structural Study of the Western*. Berkeley: University of California Press.

Youngerman, Suzanne. 1974. "Curt Sachs and His Heritage: A Critical Review of 'World History of the Dance' with a Survey of Recent Studies That Perpetuate His Ideas." *CORD News* 6(2):6–19.

Youngerman, Suzanne. 1983. "'Shaking Is No Foolish Play': An Anthropological Perspective on the American Shakers—Person, Time, Space, and Dance-Ritual." Ph.D. dissertation, Columbia University.

Zientara, Jerry. 1980. "Notes on 'Dance as Art-Sport.'" Unpublished manuscript.

Zimmer, Elizabeth. 1983. "Working the Room." *Village Voice* (27 December):106.

Films and Videotapes

These videotapes are available for viewing by the public at the Lincoln Center Library for the Performing Arts in New York City or can be obtained from Contact Collaborations, Inc.

"Chute." 1978. Contact Collaborations, Inc.

"Contact at 10th and 2nd." 1983. Contact Collaborations, Inc.

"Contact Improvisation." 1978. Northampton, Massachusetts.

"Fall After Newton: Contact Improvisation 1972–83." 1988. Contact Collaborations, Inc.

"Magnesium." 1978. Contact Collaborations, Inc.

"Soft Pallet." 1978. Contact Collaborations, Inc.

"Steve Paxton: The Judson Project." 1983. Bennington College, Vermont.

Index